REDEFINING DESIGNING

FROM FORM
TO
EXPERIENCE

C. THOMAS MITCHELL

VNR VAN NOSTRAND REINHOLD
_____ New York

COVER ILLUSTRATIONS FROM: BRIAN ENO, INSTALLATION SERIES
FRONT—#9 Three moments from "SMALL PASTURES" (San Francisco, 1988). Approximately 2 metres wide.
BACK—#2 A moment from "VENICE 3" (Venice, 1985). One of a group of five pieces, each 120cm x 30cm, and each independently illuminated by a 20" TV monitor.
Photos: Jeffrey Newbury / Atelier Markgraph. © OPAL INFORMATION

Library of Congress Catalog Card Number 92-36637
ISBN 0-442-00987-6

I(T)P Van Nostrand Reinhold is an International Thomson Publishing company.
ITP logo is a trademark under license.

Van Nostrand Reinhold
115 Fifth Avenue
New York, NY 10003

International Thomson Publishing GmbH
Königswinterer Str. 418
53227 Bonn
Germany

International Thomson Publishing
Berkshire House,168-173
High Holborn, London WC1V 7AA
England

International Thomson Publishing Asia
221 Henderson Bldg. #05-1
Singapore 0315

Thomas Nelson Australia
102 Dodds Street
South Melbourne 3205
Victoria, Australia

International Thomson Publishing Japan
Kyowa Building, 3F
2-2-1 Hirakawacho
Chiyoda-Ku, Tokyo 102
Japan

Nelson Canada
1120 Birchmount Road
Scarborough, Ontario
M1K 5G4, Canada

16 15 14 13 12 11 10 9 8 7 6 5 4 3 2

Library of Congress Cataloging-in-Publication Data

Mitchell, C. Thomas.
        Redefining designing : from form to experience / by C. Thomas Mitchell.
                p.   cm.
        Includes index.
        ISBN 0-442-00987-9
        1. Architectural design. 2. Architecture—human factors. I. Title.
NA2750.M56   1993
729—dc20   92-36637
                                                    CIP

REDEFINING DESIGNING

FROM FORM

TO

EXPERIENCE

To Chris and Claire

CONTENTS

ACKNOWLEDGMENTS

This is a collaborative book, reflecting the input and ideas of many people. I would like to briefly acknowledge some of those without whom this book could not have been written.

I would first like to thank those professors who originally motivated me to explore alternative approaches to design during my undergraduate studies of architecture: George Conley, Al DeLong, Joe Kersavage, and Walter Shouse. I would also like to thank my doctoral thesis supervisors, Roy Davis and Martin Froy, who compelled me to refine my thinking, researching, and writing. Thanks too to John Thackara for his advice and encourgement.

The help of the librarians and the resources of Indiana University have been essential to me in writing this book. I am also very grateful for the ongoing support of my department chair, Kate Rowold.

I would like to express my appreciation to the many people, publishers, and firms who have kindly consented to let me reproduce their writings and images in my book. Central to this book are the contributions of a number of leading designers, artists, and theorists. In particular I would like to express my deep gratitude to Christopher Alexander, Christo and Jeanne-Claude Christo, Brian Eno, and John Rheinfrank for their generous help with this project, though none of these people have seen, or necessarily agree with, my overall analysis and conclusions. Thanks also to Jane at Opal, Ltd. for her patient assistance.

The editors and staff at Van Nostrand Reinhold have all been extremely helpful and I would like to thank in particular Kevin Callahan for his care and thought in producing this book.

The book is based on the ideas of John Chris Jones, which have guided the development of my thinking on design. I am particularly thankful to Chris, who has been intimately involved in the book's development from the outset, giving his time and insights freely and providing invaluable critical comments throughout the conceptualizing, researching, writing, and editing of this book.

To conclude, I would like to thank my wife, Claire, who has lived with this book's gradual, and sometimes painful, evolution. Throughout the process she has been extremely supportive, tolerant, and helpful, though no doubt by this stage she never wishes to hear the words *the book* again.

My sincere thanks to you all.

INTRODUCTION

Just over a decade ago I entered architecture school with no particular preconceptions about the nature of the field, either in education or in practice. I was, however, surprised at the extent to which the design methods taught focused almost exclusively on the manipulation of geometrical forms on drawings with only the scantest attention to the needs of the eventual design users.

At the time I entered architecture school there was growing public dissatisfaction with the profession in the wake of a range of well publicized building failures — buildings that had been given awards by the architectural profession but that failed to suit the purposes for which they were intended. I am not referring here to physical or structural failures, but rather to cases in which buildings have failed the test of use.

The most publicized failure of award-winning architecture is Minoru Yamasaki's Pruitt-Igoe public housing project in St. Louis, which was designed in 1951 and destroyed in 1972 at the tenants' request, due to the building's total unsuitability for the users' needs.[1] Much has been written about this project, perhaps too much, but it is worth mentioning again because it clearly reflects the position in which the architectural community has placed itself with regard to public criticisms and concerns — the ostrich position. The more professionally oriented instructors in my architecture school informed students that the architectural design of Pruitt-Igoe had not really been a failure at all but instead had simply been the subject of an ill-informed media attack. Pruitt-Igoe failed, we were told, because the residents were not sophisticated enough to live in an award-winning building.

Pruitt-Igoe was not a unique failure but rather one in a regular sequence of recent buildings that have proven to be social failures. This trend continues, as seen in the controversy surrounding the recently completed award-winning design of the State of Illinois Center in Chicago by Helmut Jahn. Among other complaints about Jahn's building made by those who must use it are that the building's huge expanses of south-facing glass make it almost impossible to heat and cool properly. During the summer, for example, occupants have had to endure temperatures of 95°F and higher *inside* the building. In addition to the climate-control difficulties, noise generated in the building's large, open atrium penetrates the open-plan offices above it and makes them difficult to work in. Workers also complain of a lack of privacy and many suffer from acrophobia due to the height of the open atrium "void" and its proximity to their

Richard Meier
and Associates.
**Bronx Development
Center, New York, 1976.
Exterior view.**
The client's brief called
for a "warm, homelike
atmosphere."

workspaces.[2] *Chicago Tribune* critic Paul Gapp, who is otherwise sympathetic to the building, reports: "Its functional problems are also turning it into a textbook example of architecture that is scandalously short on user comfort."[3] These various examples of the social failure of architectural design result from the remoteness of the architect's design criteria and methods from the needs and wishes of design users.

The gulf between the work of architects and the needs of the publics they are to serve was most clearly illustrated to me, while I was still an architecture student, by the case of the Bronx Development Center, a four-story shiny aluminum building by Richard Meier and Associates that was completed in 1976. The building, which was to house mentally deficient children in a "warm, home-like atmosphere," was given a wide range of architectural awards including an Honor Award for design excellence, a Bartlett Award for architecture for the handicapped, and a R.S. Reynolds Award for distinguished architecture using aluminum, all from the American Institute of Architects. It also received a Bard Award for excellence in architecture and urban design from the City Club of New York. It should be noted that all of these awards were given in 1977, over a year *before* the building was occupied. The fact that a building for the mentally deficient would be judged an example of "architectural excellence" or "ready accessibility for the handicapped" — to cite just two of the awards' criteria — before being occupied vividly demonstrates the divorce of architects' concerns from those of design users.

The descriptions of the Bronx Development Center in the architectural journals, all made before the building was occupied, reveal that architects are often more concerned with formal beauty than with the satisfaction of user requirements. I will quote from these accounts at length, from a wide variety of sources, to demonstrate that I have not been overly selective in my choice of quotations but rather that I am reflecting a broad consensus among writers in the architectural press. Ada Louise Huxtable, a Pulitzer Prize-winning architecture critic, wrote a *New York Times* article about the Bronx Development Center that was titled — perhaps with unintentional irony — "A Landmark Before Its Doors Open." She writes of the building that:

**Richard Meier
and Associates.
Bronx Development
Center, New York, 1976.
Exterior view.**
A view of the "gleaming
aluminum skin."

There are some buildings that the world watches and some buildings that the profession watches, and one of the most watched by architects right now is the Bronx Development Center by Richard Meier and Associates. . . . While it waits for those pathetic shards of humanity and the severely retarded and handicapped of the Bronx who are eligible for this state institution, the structure has become the cynosure of the architectural world. . . . As the first large-scale public work of one of the most talented younger American architects, the Bronx Development Center deserves the attention it is getting. Until now, Richard Meier has been known for a series of pristine white houses of complex and sophisticated artistry. This structure goes far beyond those elegant exercises in abstract synthesis and historical recall. It has become a catalyst for some of today's more progressive trends in architectural practice. But most of all, the new building stands on its own, and on its merits, as a distinguished work of art.[4]

Another critic, Stanley Abercrombie, says the building is "remarkable, extraordinary, dazzling. The gleaming aluminum skin, the carefully placed elements, the play of geometry — all this, from the outside, is superb. We automatically reach for our cameras."[5] In an article written just after the completion of the Bronx Development Center, Suzanne Stephens says:

[T]he individual architect, with his invincible faith in pure lofty ideals, his adherence to the standards of quality as he rises above the morass of mediocrity in the built environment, still arouses professional and public longing. If the *morality* of Modernism's functionalist credos is no longer the crucial issue, a new kind of morality has sprouted up around architecture's formal and aesthetic obligations.

Of this breed Richard Meier might be the purest and most prolific representative in terms of translating ideas into built form. The haunting evocative quality of his kind of formalism — not too cerebral, not too polemical — appeals to a public that has often seen the modernist aesthetic, but not in a refined, rarefied state. Faced with the limitless erosion of quality in daily life, the desire for a setting that transcends all by the sheer force of its incorruptible belief system can secretly possess the most realistic of souls. The astringency and purity of form, the rigor of a superb composition of unswerving discipline can be painfully seductive to the most pragmatic psyche. Not to be ignored of course is the status-conferring powers of pure form. Sign of enlightened, noncommercial values, architecture-as-art-object attest to the client's own powers of sensitivity, understanding and cultivation.

. . . His success has been enviable: published, awarded, and copied. Meier's work has placed him in the forefront of architectural effort . . . he has proved that it is still possible to create Architecture — the kind of environment that is more than "nicely designed," the kind of environment that lets you know that Architecture as a special category lives.[6]

It is clear from their comments that these critics believe that the "architectural quality" of Meier's work, its status as a formal art object, can be considered independently of its suitability for the purpose for which it was intended. To them the success of architecture, as in the case of the Bronx Development Center, can be judged before the building has been used at all. When architecture is considered a formal art it is not conceived with design users in mind but rather is practiced for the benefit of the architect's own peer group: other architects, the architectural press, and the juries of the architectural awards (and there is a great deal of overlap among these groups).

The attitude of the architectural press toward the mentally deficient children who were the end users of the Bronx Development Center is remarkably patronizing, a "let them eat cake, if they know how" approach. An article in *Architectural Review*, for example, reassures us: "It will be difficult for the patients to feel that they are anywhere but inside an institution. But at least they can be comforted by the knowledge that they inhabit an extremely refined example of architectural design."[7] Is the anonymous reviewer here seriously suggesting that children who require institutionalization will be able to appreciate, much less be comforted by, "an extremely refined example of architectural design"?

Paul Goldberger, another Pulitzer Prize-winning critic, similarly writes: "Here, an architect has practiced his art with immense sensitivity. . . . What that process has yielded is a building that is serene and beautiful to sophisticated eyes; one can only hope that to its occupants it will appear the same."[8] Is Goldberger saying that the mentally deficient *will* perceive the building in the same way as those with "sophisticated eyes"? Or rather is he saying that if they do not then their opinions do not matter anyway?

The principal concern of the architectural press seems to be the elevation of architecture to an art form — adopting the view that buildings are formal art objects frozen in space. Even granting that architecture can be viewed as a formal art, one can still investigate the degree to which a resulting building fulfills the criteria given the architect by the client. In the case of the Bronx Development Center the client, the Facilities Development Corporation of the State of New York, asked that the building have a "warm, homelike atmosphere"[9] for the residents. To what extent did Meier achieve, or even attempt, to realize this quality? The first thing he did was "interpret" the brief, transforming the client's given — and to the layperson, understandable — criteria, into his own

**Richard Meier
and Associates**.
**Bronx Development
Center, New York, 1976.
Interior view.**
Meier's aim was to
"create a sense of place
that responds to the
special feelings and
needs of the residents."

more ambiguous one, "a sense of place." As Meier himself says, "While the program's complex technical requirements demanded particular attention, the design is above all an attempt to create a sense of place that responds to the special feelings and needs of the residents."[10] In transforming the brief Meier rejects the client's own criteria and substitutes instead his own formal concerns. In so doing Meier makes himself the sole judge of the "special feelings and needs" of the center's residents, a sleight of hand that is a commonplace in the architectural profession. Not surprisingly the architectural community supports his substitution of "sense of place" for the client's own criteria, "a warm, homelike atmosphere." The jurors who voted the building an AIA Honor Award say of it:

The strategy was to have the complex open inward, protecting the children from the ugliness of the outside world. Despite the fact that intricate scientific and technical functions and procedures had to be given major consideration, the designers gave equal priority to the creation of a "sense of place" for the special needs of the users.[11]

This comment is, strangely, almost identical to Meier's statement of his design intentions. The way in which the "sense of place" was created and the jurors' criteria for judging its success in the as yet unoccupied building are left unspecified.

Those outside the architectural community were highly critical of the building. For example, according to New York state assemblyman Guy V. Vallela, who investigated the Center, "This place is a fiasco. . . . It won all sorts of awards for beautiful design, but it's totally unsuited for the purpose for which it was intended."[12] The architectural press, however, dismissed these ill-informed opinions. Ada Louis Huxtable, for example, wrote: "Criticism of the design centers on expressions of concern about an 'unhomelike' atmosphere, but *the architect's emphasis* [my italics] is more on the human scale of the rooms and their arrangement than on a familiar ambience." She goes on to make a startling admission: "No one really knows about the effect of design quality," but she then falls back on the architect's own explanation, "but the intent is to create a 'comfortable' physical and psychic atmosphere."[13] Again, no indication is given as to how this was, or was to have been, achieved.

Architecture critic Suzanne Stephens also addressed the public's reaction to the building:

The most controversial issue in the Bronx case concerns the center's intended "homelike" quality. Although furniture has not yet been moved in, making it difficult to visualize how "homelike" the center will be, a considerable amount of criticism has already been leveled at the scheme for not looking anything like a home. . . . The program for the Bronx Developmental Center called for a "warm homelike atmosphere" (home-type finishes) in the residential units. . . . The cool detached mien strikes many as beautiful, calming, salubrious, rational, recalling the utopian promise of Modern Architecture. The lay public often sees it as strange, off-putting, frightening — an impression that may or may not change with time.

From these reactions two questions emerge: Is a "homelike" exterior a tenable architectural criterion? Second, will its users, the mentally retarded, perceive it the same way as parents, architects, general public and so on? Since they have not yet occupied the center, their reactions can't be observed, and little scientific evidence exists that explicitly describes how the mentally retarded respond to architecture, much less *this* architecture. Will they be alienated by the aluminum skin or be attracted to this bright shiny surface? Will they perceive the place as an institution or as a community? Are these the right questions to ask of their perceptions in the first place?[14]

Stephens is to be credited for determining a range of very correct questions to ask with regard to a building for the mentally deficient, though by the time she raised them the point was moot since the building was already completed, albeit unoccupied. Perhaps unintentionally she raises a very important point here: no one *does* know how people, any people, will react to architecture. But this again raises the question of how the Bronx Development Center could have been judged an unqualified success in the first place by the architectural community with so many issues left unresolved.

We may not be able finally to conclude the extent to which Meier's building is or is not warm and homelike, but we can perhaps determine the degree to which he concerned himself with the client's particular needs by comparing his design for the Bronx Development Center to those of his other buildings for other purposes. Reviews by a range of architecture critics praise the fact that Meier's work is "consistent," that is, the formal language he uses — the design elements and appearance — is common to all his buildings whether single family houses for wealthy clients, monumental public buildings such as designs for museums and corporate headquarters, or an institution for the mentally deficient. The principal focus of the critics is, as always, on the formal properties of the building, though some grudging acknowledgment of the client's program is given.

Suzanne Stephens says: "In terms of architectural problem-solving, the building is clearly a masterpiece, one of refinement, not invention. . . . There is no disintegration of the idea when the form meets the demands of a complicated program."[15] Paul Goldberger is a bit more circumspect:

Mr. Meier's well-known "white" houses show that he is a superb maker of compositions, and this is surely his finest composition ever. Such aspects of this building as the view from the two-story lobby into the courtyard, where a freestanding outside stair perfectly balances its opposite number inside are architectural experiences of a truly high order. But what it comes down to is if the stylistic vocabulary at use here is the correct one for this most unusual and troubling of architectural challenges.[16]

Stanley Abercrombie views the building as a formal success on the one hand and a $40-million experiment on the other:

The Bronx center . . . is actually severe, uncompromising, consistent, and intellectually rigorous in its mechanization. Perhaps more than any other building of our time, it attempts to affirm the architect as God. Whether this attitude is the one most appropriate in an institution for the mentally retarded . . . may perhaps be partly answered as mental health experts watch the building in use.[17]

So we see from the critics' comments that Meier did not vary his own work practices to suit the client's particular program, but rather adapted and "interpreted" the program in such a way that it would conform to the formal approach he uses in all of his work. Individual commissions can then be viewed not as opportunities to find the best solution to a client's program but rather as occasions to further one's own experiments with form. In this sense variations in building types and client programs are incidental to the architect's real task — pure formal composition.

The cladding material chosen for the Bronx Development Center — shiny aluminum panels — differs slightly from the white anodized panels used in most of Meier's previous work. This decision, however, raises the issue of whether this switch of materials was made in an attempt to fulfill the client's request that the building have a warm, homelike feel. The architectural press again addresses solely the formal aspects of Meier's decision. For example, Ada Louis Huxtable states:

The whole project is marked by an extremely disciplined interlocking of logic and art. Meier's move from white to silver is also a move to maturity. In spite of its fashionably "minimalist" components, this building has a richness of composition and a finesse and originality of form that mark an important new phase in architectural design.[18]

The anonymous author of an article in *Industrial Design* did admit that "Though its bold, machined look and intelligent planning have indeed found general appeal among professionals, some laymen find its atmosphere 'alienating'."[19] The layperson's impression of the building, while mentioned, is not acknowledged to have any value; instead the word *alienating* is placed in quotation marks like a word whose meaning is foreign or utterly obscure.

It is becoming clear that the views of architects, with their almost exclusive focus on architecture as a formal art, differ from those of most everyone else. Furthermore, to a great extent the architect's approach excludes other peoples' views from consideration in the design process — not just the users' viewpoint, but the client's as well. This discrepancy in viewpoints was made most vivid in the *New York Times*. In different parts of the same newspaper, one could read two radically different accounts of the Bronx Development Center, one a glowing assessment of the *architecture* of the building, the other a scathing account of the building's total unsuitability for its purpose. In "Masterwork or Nightmare?" Paul Goldberger acknowledged both sides of the story — the architecture community's view and that of people concerned for the users. He cited two typical contrasting opinions:

"This is a place of refuge, a sanctuary," said John Hejuk, dean of the school of architecture at Cooper Union, of the new Bronx Development Center designed by Richard Meier. To Mr. Hejuk, the center — a long, low building sheathed in aluminum panels — is a "masterwork," a place where "architecture can lift up the spirit and make life a little better." To Anthony Pitto, a parent active in the parents' organization of the Willowbrook State School for the retarded, the new building is "an architect's nightmare of a submarine".[20]

Hejuk's judgment is based on the architect's criteria — architecture as art — while Pitto's judgment is based on the suitability of the building for the intended use, to house mentally retarded children. As is so often the case the architect's judgments are antithetical to those of the people who must live with their designs.

Another view of the Bronx Development Center sanctioned by the architectural community is put forward in an article by Stanley Abercrombie:

Richard Meier's Bronx Development Center is one of the most honored buildings of our time, yet only now is it beginning to be put to use in the rehabilitation of the mentally retarded. In fact, its honors . . . have been rather controversial, for some have questioned whether an unoccupied shell should ever be judged excellent architecture. But in October of 1977, approximately a year after the building's completion, the first day care patients were admitted to the center, and the first residential patients were accepted in mid-June of 1978. As of the first of November, 28 patients were living and sleeping in the facility — far from the built capacity of 380, but the plans are now that the number will gradually increase.[21]

Not deterred by the indications that there may be major problems with the building, Abercrombie continues:

Not only do the interiors work; they sing. Most obviously, they sing with color — some pastels, some primaries, some deep and vibrant. Although the rest of the building is characterized by order, the distribution of color seems to be purely subjective and uncoded. "We know the retarded react strongly to color," Meier says, "but we don't know exactly how. There is no definite research about their responses." The building, he thinks, may afford "a way of testing" such responses. In a more important (and more permanent) way, the Bronx center sings with logic and order. If "Euclid alone has looked on Beauty bare," Meier has been peeking over Euclid's shoulder. In its rationality — what some might now, eight years after its design, consider *excessive* rationality — the building may well be the apex — both the culmination and the turning point — of an important direction in this century's architecture: the attempt at complete subjugation of the environment to human will.

The use of major spaces as events in the basic circulation routes, the manipulation of views across the courtyard, and even the length and straightness of the corridors — all contribute to the remarkable degree to which a user or visitor is led by Meier to *understand* the building, and who can doubt that such understanding of one's environment can be beneficially supportive? The Bronx Development Center, as was widely recognized, was an important building even before occupancy. As an ultimate testing ground of the relationship between architectural order and human response, it is even more important as a building in use.[22]

Abercrombie suggests the Bronx Development Center is a grand (but does not mention greatly expensive) experiment, though no testing method for the experiment is identified. He assures us that the experiment will be a success, going so far as to ask, "Who can doubt that such an understanding of one's environment can be beneficially supportive?" making the implicit assumption that the users of the center *would* understand the building in the way Meier intended. If we do accept Abercrombie's contention that the Bronx Development Center was the "ultimate testing ground of the relationship between architectural order and human response" then what were the results of the test? According to Dr. James Clements, director of the Georgia Retardation Center in Atlanta, the Bronx Development Center "represents the wrong concept at the wrong time in the wrong place."[23]

An article in the *New York Times*, though not in the "Architecture View" section, explained:

The Bronx Development Center, a $40 million state facility completed four years ago to house retarded children, still lacks a fire alarm system connected to the New York City Fire Department and has several other safety hazards, parents and other witnesses told a State Senate hearing yesterday. . . . Among the improvements scheduled . . . are installation of shatterproof glass on windows in areas used by patients, enclosing of exterior fire stairs and interior stairwell landings and increasing the height of safety railings.[24]

The article goes on to say that a moratorium on admissions to the center was imposed "that has held the number of residential patients to 180 — less than half the 384 bed capacity — until safety measures were completed and the staff increased."[25]

But didn't the American Institute of Architects give the building not just an Honor Award but also a Bartlett Award for design for the handicapped? The awards jury said of the Center: "Designed for the handicapped, the buildings provide handrails, ramps for wheelchairs and light switches lower than the usual height, as well as other amenities to help make life easier for the residents."[26] Not easy enough, clearly. Once the architect had interpreted the brief, thus making himself the sole judge of the residents' "special feelings and needs," he was free to operate in complete ignorance of the users' real require-ments. More disturbing still is that a jury representing the American Institute of Architects and empowered to grant an award for handicapped accessible design apparently didn't understand the needs of the handicapped users either.

The *New York Times* article on the safety problems of the center concluded: "The Bronx Developmental Center, whose four-story-high walls of sheet alu-minum make it a landmark in an otherwise dreary industrial section, is not the only recent public facility to win praise for its architectural design while prompting criticism from its intended users."[27]

Criticisms of the Bronx Development Center was met with denial in the architectural community. An article in the *AIA Journal*, for example, says of the center:

It and the awards have been widely, but not unanimously, criticized by mental health pro-fessionals (and architects specializing in mental health facilities) — not for its design but for the fact that the center concentrates so many patients in a single institution instead of their being treated in smaller facilities thoroughly integrated in the community.[28]

It is true that changes in attitude toward care for the mentally deficient were taking place during the time the building was designed and built, and that this caused changes in the building's program. But whatever philosophy of care for the mentally ill is adopted it seems reasonable to expect a $40-million award-winning public building at least to be safe!

Suzanne Stephens reveals that the Willowbrook plaintiffs, a group of parents whose children would be housed in the Bronx Development Center, contended:

The building is unsafe, a restrictive environment, and not "homelike." The unsafe fea-tures alluded to include items such as open railings, open tread stairs, an open bridge, the use of untempered glass in many areas, and some unguarded drops in the courtyard. Already the architects are designing wire infill for the railings, steel plate treads for the lobby stair, and making other *small* [my italics] adjustments.[29]

Is it that the architect did not know that these features were unsafe and unsuitable? Or did formal considerations overshadow all others? After all, these design features are present in most of Meier's work. A lack of sensitivity to the needs of the residents is the corollary in this case to the purity and consistency of the formal language Meier uses. It is extremely ironic that a building so unsuitable to its purpose was so often praised for its "sensitive detailing."

What was the architect's reaction to the controversy surrounding his award-winning building? To judge from his book *Richard Meier Architect*, published in 1984, eight years after the completion of the building, there was no controversy. The book devoted twenty-three pages to the building and the only information about reaction to the building is contained in the caption of a glossy photograph:

Once when this building was nearing completion, a carload of people drove up and asked whether they could live here. When told it was a facility for the mentally disabled, they said they would like to apply for a job. To the architect this seemed a great compli-ment in terms of the intention to create a livable and appealing environment.[30]

Richard Meier and Associates. Bronx Development Center, New York, 1976. Interior view. A view of the open stairwells, railings, and expanses of glass that were considered to be safety problems and that had to be modified by the architects.

The book never mentions whether this group of well-wishers ever actually went *inside* the building but we can assume they were neither mentally retarded nor ever lived there, so their judgment — and the architect's interpretation of it — seems to be as ill founded as the opinions many architects and their supporters like to generate to obscure their disregard of user needs. By the time of the book's publication there was ample evidence that the building was not a "livable and appealing environment."

Stephens writes of the controversy surrounding the building that "These sticky legal issues have little to do with the architectural design of Bronx Development Center, for according to this line of reasoning even the Taj Mahal would be turned down."[31] Taking her assertions in turn, if a building is unsafe owing to poor design then it would seem to have *everything* to do with its architectural design. Stephens further implies, as is now familiar, that the architectural design of the center can somehow be considered in isolation from the context of its use. Finally, "the Taj Mahal would be turned down," not because of such mundane considerations as safety, but rather because its form is not designed to cater to the needs of the users of a mental health center; though from what we have seen it is probably true that the Taj Mahal would be no less suitable as a mental health center than is the Bronx Development Center.

Having reviewed all the evidence against the center, Stephens still could not stray from the party line:

To reject the center is to reject the timeless architectural principles it so splendidly embodies, the worthwhile modernist notions it has staunchly upheld. Despite the ambivalence, the controversy, the diverse reactions to the Bronx Development Center, the building will no doubt become an important historical landmark. In the final analysis the design is about architecture and its possibilities, qualities that will endure once the circumstances of its difficult birth are forgotten.[32]

I would agree with Stephens that the Bronx Development Center should become an important historical landmark, but as a symbol not of formal beauty but of the insidious disregard of user needs, all the worse in this case because of the vulnerability of the users who will not have an opportunity to "vote with their feet" if they find Meier's "masterpiece" not to their liking. I would also agree that "the design is about architecture and its possibilities," with the design clearly illustrating the extremely limited possibility of present architectural methods creating designs that suit the needs and wishes of users and clients. But I question whether the Bronx Development Center embodies "timeless architectural principles" or whether it instead represents the simplification of the architectural task in the twentieth century to a focus on geometrical criteria alone, to the exclusion of meaningful consideration of user needs and client requirements.

I would like to make clear that I am not questioning the formal beauty of the Bronx Development Center — I find the building visually very exciting. What I *am* questioning is the seemingly exclusive reliance on visual criteria for such a complex building task, to the apparent exclusion of meaningful consideration of the building's users. It is also important to emphasize that I am not questioning the central importance of art in creating user-sensitive designs; rather I am suggesting that architects may have chosen the wrong forms of art to emulate. I am opposed to the mistaken identification of architecture with the static, visual criteria of the plastic arts, instead of with the dynamic, multisensory nature of the "time arts." Theater, or performance art generally, provides a much better model than two-dimensional drawings, or even sculpture, for the way in which designs are experienced and used.

There are few cases in design like the Bronx Development Center in which the user group has such specifically definable needs and such a lack of adaptability to cope with design errors. In most cases it is more true to speak of user wishes, rather than needs, as most people have a remarkable ability to adjust even to the worst designs. In fact, many people are aware of design only when it interrupts their routines and do not consciously think about it at other times. No one should be forced to adapt to bad design, but to produce a design for a vulnerable population without ensuring that it is suitable for their needs is surely the wrong approach.

Some may suggest that the failure of the Bronx Development Center is linked to the building's being designed in the late modernist style, a movement that focuses on the forms of the modern movement while eschewing modernism's moral purpose. The lack of correspondence between the architect's means and user needs, however, as will be discussed in a subsequent chapter, is common to all design movements since industrialization: modernism, late modernism, deconstruction, and postmodernism (whose adherents acknowledge users' "taste codes" but only as a stylistic device).

The proliferation of cases of architectural failures such as the Bronx Development Center led me, while still a student of architecture, to the inescapable conclusion that architects, whether they personally care about user requirements or not, do not actually know how users will react to designs. Further, architects do not have any meaningful methods for ascertaining and designing for user requirements.

There has been a ground swell of popular criticism of architects, most notably Tom Wolfe's *From Bauhaus to Our House*[33] and Prince Charles's ongoing pronouncements on the subject.[34] While their criticisms of recent trends in architecture might be sound, they give architects entirely too much credit for being able to find a way out of their present malaise, implying that a change of priorities *within* architectural design methods would be sufficient to put things right — to achieve a proper relationship between architect and users. Wolfe and the prince seem to feel that a change in the visual appearance of buildings is all that is needed correct the recent failures in architecture; in so doing they mistake style for substance and style for design. Traditional methods of design, which focus almost exclusively on the manipulation of geometrical forms, are inapplicable to design in which users' wishes and needs are the principal focus. The problems with architecture today cannot be solved from within using traditional architectural design methods; rather the methods of design themselves must change.

My intent has not been to jump on the already crowded "bash architects and architecture" bandwagon, but rather to attempt to demonstrate, using architecture as an example, why so many designs fail the test of use. What follows is an analysis of the changing nature of design in the postindustrial era, a survey of the responsiveness of contemporary design movements to the needs of users, a review of the development of processes and methods of design that explicitly address the needs of users, cases studies of user-sensitive design approaches, and a redefinition of design in terms of user experience, not physical form.

REDEFINING DESIGNING

FROM FORM
TO
EXPERIENCE

PART 1
DESIGN IN TRANSITION

Over the past few decades, the industrial age has been giving way to a postindustrial era. This transition has profound consequences, throwing into question most traditional notions of what design is and what designers do. New technological developments, for example, are making it possible for design to become much more responsive to the cultural, social, and personal needs of design users than had been the case in the industrial era. The distinguishing characteristic of the emerging postindustrial tasks is that designing is more focused on the dynamic processes of user experience than on physical form. Tracing the transition from the product-based design of the industrial age to the more process-based design of the postindustrial era, Italian designer and theorist Andrea Branzi observes:

Classical design always referred to mass markets, and these are now disappearing. This is partly because standardization, with its urge to transform different types of behaviour and traditions into fixed universal models, had its roots in the existence of a large, homogeneous international market. Design was thus involved in thinking up objects that would suit everyone, whereas in fact they were also unsuited to everyone. These were products that were indiscriminately promoted throughout the whole range of the market.[1]

In place of the mass markets of the industrial age Branzi found instead a:

new kind of production, given the name post-industrial by theoreticians, in which the all-embracing logic of mass-production, which represses changes in taste as an unpredictable and irrational variable, was giving way to a search for flexibility. It was no longer society that must resemble the factory in every way, but the factory that had to try to adapt to society.[2]

Branzi further notes that, "design today . . . operates within a number of processes of change that lie completely outside the traditional activity of the formal and physical design of objects, in order to move forward into the world of services, to the interchange of information."[3] Design is now, as John Thackara says, "beyond the object."[4]

The character of postindustrial technology is described by design educator Charles L. Owen who writes:

It is now frequently possible to produce profitably in extremely small lots — *even lots of 1!*

The impact of this on design will be revolutionary. Among other things, it will mean substitution for the design of single products, the design of *rule systems* for families of products. Within this concept, products can be individually tailored *in the production process*, to the needs of purchasers. The conversion of the design process from the design of individual products to the design of rule systems for *product classes* will allow this individualization to take place while remaining within the intent and control of the designer. The design technology to make this possible is among the highest priorities for design research and will distinguish design in the information age.[5]

Not surprisingly, perhaps, the Japanese have been among the first to develop advanced postindustrial design approaches. A recently developed design trend in Japanese industry known as "The Human Age" is an attempt to respond to the changing nature of the design process by focusing upon the processes of using products, rather than the technology that goes into them. In an essay addressing this theme Bill Evans writes:

Without exception, all the major [Japanese] companies are developing a sophisticated analysis of the future which is becoming increasingly user conscious. They are looking to a period when advances in electronics are consolidating rather than rapidly advancing. As Ricoh puts it: "We have moved from the hardware age (1965–1975), through the software age (1975–1985) towards the humanware age." By this they mean that users' requirements will take over as the major dictator of product capability. "We have the technology" — so the companies are now concentrating on allowing designers to input consumer lifestyle into the products, making the technology more intelligent and more flexible for users of different cultural backgrounds, and generally considering the social context. . . . Many companies say, "You have to know people first before making any product."[6]

The adoption of the human-age design philosophy in Japan is now being reflected in advertising slogans. Nissan cars, for example, are "designed for the human race" and a Canon camera is "so advanced . . . it's simple."

The character of postindustrial technology differs markedly from that of the industrial age but is, surprisingly, very similar to that advocated by William Morris in the nineteenth century. Morris, an outspoken critic of industrialization and a founder of the influential Arts and Crafts movement, wrote, "It is allowing machines to be our masters and not our servants that so injures the beauty of life nowadays."[7] As an alternative to the gauche mass-produced products of the early industrial era, Morris advocated the use of handicrafts. Now technology has developed to the point at which the most advanced products are beginning to have the character of handicrafts — high quality, well adapted to their contexts of use, and even customized or individualized. As architectural critic Charles Jencks observes:

The new technologies stemming from the computer have made possible a new facility of production. This emergent type is much more geared to change and individuality than the relatively stereotyped productive processes of the First Industrial Revolution. And mass-production, mass-repetition, was of course one of the unshakable foundations of Modern Architecture. This has cracked apart, if not crumbled. For computer modelling, automated-production, and the sophisticated techniques of market research and prediction now allow us to mass-produce a variety of styles and almost personalized products. The results are closer to nineteenth-century handicraft than the regimented superblocks of 1965.[8]

As Jencks indicates, as technology becomes increasingly sophisticated it ironically becomes less rigid. The transition from the industrial age to the postindustrial era, however, is still in its incipient stages and while the development of technology provides the opportunity to create a design process more responsive to users, this is by no means guaranteed. Most discussion thus far of design in the postindustrial era centers on the opportunities for designers to enhance their professional positions, *not* on the possibility of making design more responsive to user needs and wishes. Similarly, where new technologies, such as computer-aided design, have been introduced into the design process they have been used, for the most part, in ways that *reinforce* rather than challenge exisiting design practices. The transition to the postindustrial has necessitated a change in the focus of the design process from physical form to users' experience, from mass production to custom adaptation, and — to paraphrase Morris — from having machines, and industrial technologies generally, be our masters to having them be our servants.

1. Design Philosophies Since Industrialization

From the outset, it might be instructive to determine the extent to which the principal design approaches of the present and recent past have succeeded or failed in producing user-responsive designs. Particularly relevant is an exploration of the principal design approach developed in response to the onset of industrialization — modernism — and the range of more recent reactions to and against modernism, including postmodernism, late modernism, deconstruction, and the notion of the second modernity. The presence of these various ideas in the work of architects will be examined to determine the extent to which they have or have not helped realize designs that are responsive to the needs and wishes of design users.

MODERNISM

Contemporary design movements, whatever their ideological differences, can all be seen as reactions (or reactions to reactions) to the process of industrialization. In this sense modernism, postmodernism, late modernism, deconstruction, and the second modernity, though vastly differing approaches, are all attempts to come to terms with a world that is, at least potentially, dominated by the machine.

The first major reaction of the design community to the industrial revolution was the modern movement. One of the major aims of the movement was to develop means of providing decent, basic housing for large numbers of workers. The modernists were heavily influenced by the ideas of William Morris, who had written, "I don't want art for a few, any more than education for a few, what business have we with art at all unless all can share it?"[1] Unlike Morris, however, the moderns were willing to embrace, rather than reject, industrial technology to realize their aims. In fact, the modern architects used the process of industrialization itself as a metaphor, and within industrialization the metaphor of metaphors was the factory. Naturally enough, therefore, standardization and mass production become key tenets of the modernist philosophy of architecture.

Walter Gropius, founder of the Bauhaus in Germany, where much of modernist theory was developed, wrote:

Standardization is not an impediment to the development of civilization, but, on the contrary, one of its immediate prerequisites. A standard may be defined as that simplified practical exemplar of anything in general use which embodies a fusion of the best of its anterior forms — a fusion preceded by the elimination of the personal content of their designers and all otherwise ungeneric or non-essential features. Such an impersonal standard is called a "norm," a word derived from a carpenter's square.

The fear that individuality will be crushed out by the growing "tyranny" of standardization is the sort of myth which cannot sustain the briefest examination. In all great epochs of history the existence of standards — that is the conscious adoption of type-forms — has been the criterion of a polite, well-ordered society; for it is a commonplace that repetition of the same things for the same purposes exercises a settling and civilizing influence on men's minds.[2]

In Gropius's argument we find a blurring of categories, the existence of societal standards being used as justification for the standardization of formal components — an unproven and, in view of history, untenable assertion. This approach underpins all of Gropius's thinking. He further praises the general to the *exclusion* of the individual:

A prudent limitation of variety to a few standard types of buildings increases their quality and decreases their cost; thereby raising the social level of the population as a whole. Proper respect for tradition will find a truer echo in these than in the miscellaneous solution of an often arbitrary and aloof individualism because the greater communal utility of the former embodies a deeper architectural significance. . . .

The standardization of the practical machinery of life implies no robotization of the individual, but, on the contrary, the unburdening of his existence from much unnecessary dead-weight so as to leave him freer to develop on a higher plane. Efficient and well-oiled machinery of daily life cannot of course constitute an end in itself, but it at least forms a point of departure for the acquisition of a maximum personal freedom and independence.[3]

Gropius never, however, articulates the nature of the connection between standardizing architectural forms and liberating people to "develop on a higher plane" of freedom and independence.

The modern architects' belief in the inevitability and rightness of industrialization is clearly stated by Gropius:

It is now becoming widely recognized that although the outward forms of the New Architecture differ fundamentally in an organic sense from those of the old, they are not the personal whims of a handful of architects avid for innovation at all cost, but simply the *inevitable* [my italics] logical product of the intellectual, social and technical conditions of our age. A quarter of a century's earnest and pregnant struggle preceded their eventual emergence.[4]

Gropius was not alone in his belief that standardization and the adoption of mass production was inevitable, necessary, and morally elevating. Another of

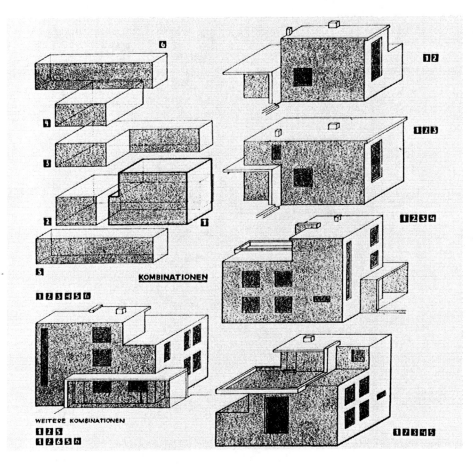

Walter Gropius. Bauhaus Housing, Weimar, 1922. "Box of Bricks" Presentation Board (detail). This project exemplifies Gropius' belief in the use of standardization and mass production as the basis of modern architecture.

the leading figures in the modern movement, Le Corbusier, similarly and unambiguously, wrote:

A great epoch has begun.

There exists a new spirit.

Industry, overwhelming us like a flood which rolls on towards its destined ends, has furnished us with new tools adapted to this new epoch, animated by the new spirit.

Economic law inevitably governs our acts and our thoughts.

The problem of the house is a problem of the epoch. The equilibrium of society today depends upon it. Architecture has for its first duty, in this period of renewal, that of bringing about a revision of values, a revision of the constituent elements of the house.

Mass-production is based on analysis and experiment.

Industry on the grand scale must occupy itself with building and establish the elements of the house on a mass-production basis.

We must create the mass-production spirit.

The spirit of constructing mass-production houses.

The spirit of living in mass-production houses.

The spirit of conceiving mass-production houses.

If we eliminate from our hearts and minds all dead concepts in regard to the house, and look at the question from a critical and objective point of view, we shall arrive at the "House-Machine", the mass-production house, healthy (and morally so too) and beauti-

**Le Corbusier.
Unite d'Habitation,
Marseilles, 1952.**
One of Le Corbusier's
"machines for living in."

ful in the same way that the working tools and instruments which accompany our existence are beautiful.

Beautiful also with all the animation that the artist's sensibility can add to severe and pure functioning elements.[5]

Le Corbusier also writes:

The Architect, by his arrangement of forms, realizes an order which is a pure creation of his spirit; by forms and shapes he affects our senses to an acute degree and provokes plastic emotions; by the relationships which he creates he wakes profound echoes in us, he gives us the measure of an order which we feel to be in accordance with that of our world, he determines the various movements of our heart and of our understanding; it is then that we experience the sense of beauty.[6]

Here Le Corbusier touches on one of the most pervasive, recurring, and misguided myths in design: the idea that the manipulation of physical form into "beautiful" compositions will *inevitably* have a beneficial effect on those who come in contact with it. I am not questioning the value of art per se, nor do I deny that many of Le Corbusier's buildings, such as his chapel at Ronchamp, are beautiful. What I *am* questioning is the implicit belief that form *directly* affects the perception of those who inhabit a building in a known, positive way. As noted earlier, no one really knows what the perceptual effects of architectural form are.

Throughout the practice of modern architecture, aesthetic beliefs led to impulses that interfered with the architects' ability to bring about a truly standardized and mass produced architecture. As David Byrne, in his film *True Stories,* says of the metal buildings common in the United States:

Metal buildings are the dream that modern architects had at the beginning of the century come true, but they themselves don't realize it. If they followed their own theories to the letter — form follows function, using mass-production techniques to make cheap things with no frills — what you end up with is a metal building! And when you look at it that way, it's beautiful. The reason no architect ever says that is because you don't need an architect to build metal buildings.[7]

So despite their rhetoric, if forced to choose, the modern architects were more concerned with architecture as an art form than with adhering to their theories.

In addition to the use of the factory metaphor and its corollaries, standardization and mass production, another basic element of modernist practice was the use of industrial materials — glass, steel, and concrete. Not only were these materials used, they were attributed with an almost mystical significance. As architect Adolf Behne wrote in 1918:

It is not the crazy caprice of a poet that glass architecture will bring a new culture. *It is a fact.* New social welfare organizations, hospitals, inventions, or technical innovations and improvements — these will not *bring a new culture* — but glass architecture will. . . . Therefore the European is right when he fears that glass architecture might become uncomfortable. Certainly it will be so. And that is not its least advantage. For first of all the European must be wrenched out of his coziness.[8]

As Behne's comments indicate, it is not simply that new materials for architecture were made available by the industrial process, but rather the desire — the implicit belief — of the modern architects that the practice of architecture could

**Le Corbusier.
Chapel of Notre-Dame-
du-Haut at Ronchamp,
1950–55.
Exterior view.**

9

**Le Corbusier.
Chapel of Notre-Dame-du-Haut at Ronchamp,
1950–1955.
Interior view.**

and should bring about a new culture. Also interesting is Behne's admission that the culture created by modern architecture would intentionally be uncomfortable and would lack coziness.

The adoption of the factory metaphor during the modern movement was extended to the architects themselves. Nikolaus Pevsner, one of the first critics to help define — rather than just comment upon — design, wrote:

The warmth and directness with which ages of craft and a more personal relationship between architect and client endowed buildings of the past may have gone for good. The architect, to represent this century of ours, must be colder, cold to keep in command of mechanized production, cold to design to the satisfaction of anonymous clients.

However, genius will find its own way even in times of overpowering collective energy, even within the medium of this new style of the twentieth century which, because it is a genuine style, as opposed to a passing fashion, is universal.[9]

Pevsner reveals a great deal about the modern movement in this short quote. We learn that designers *must* be cold and design *must* be impersonal in the modern era. The designer *must* because, according to Pevsner, modernism is as inevitable as it is inexorable — it is a "universal style" for the anonymous, "universal man," not a passing fashion for real, warm people.

To what extent, then, does the practice of modern architecture respond to the needs and wishes of design users? Or, put another way, what relationship is there between the "universal man" for whom the modern architect designed and the "man in the street" who had to live in the designs? Very little, if any. Modern architects were quite happy to champion workers as a class while disparaging them as individuals. Instead of designing for people as they were, modern architects sought, through the manipulation of physical form, to "improve," "elevate," or "reeducate" man ("man" meaning humankind as a whole, not Hans or Helga Schmidt as individuals). Addressing this point Andrea Branzi observes:

The Modern Movement was born in Europe along with the great ideologies of action for the transformation of the world. Secular responses to the Socialist revolution, they adopted its scale of operation and applied it to social problems that in the first decades of the century seemed to require, and in every case did require, revolutionary solutions. Rationalism, Fascism, Nazism, and Soviet Socialism were all born in the same climate of history and all proposed, although in widely differing forms, something no other ideology had ever done: the modification of the human race. This modification was the radical answer to problems whose solution could not help but demand extreme measures for the structural alteration of society, starting with its raw material, i.e. its individual human components.[10]

There was a consensus among the modern architects that radical change was needed in society. Le Corbusier, for example, wrote:

The machinery of Society, profoundly *out of gear*, oscillates between an amelioration, of historical importance, and a catastrophe. The primordial instinct of every human being

Gerd Arntz.
The Assembly-Line
Human Being, 1927.
The desire of some modernists to apply the factory metaphor to every aspect of life is clearly reflected in this linocut from the period.

is to assure himself of a shelter. The various classes of workers in society today *no longer have dwellings adapted to their needs; neither the artisan nor the intellectual.* It is a question of building which is at the root of the social unrest of to-day: architecture or revolution.[11]

So not only were changes in society needed but architecture was viewed, by architects at least, as the means of effecting the revolution. Art historian Robert Hughes writes that the modern architects were perhaps the first, and will almost certainly be the last, to believe "that the human animal could be morally improved, and that the means of this betterment was four walls and a roof."[12] Hughes notes that for the modern architects:

People, no less than their shelters, needed replanning. Revise the shelter and one improves the people. Reeducate the people and they will grasp the necessity — the *moral* necessity — of a new form of shelter. Walter Gropius and Mies van der Rohe in Germany, no less than Le Corbusier in France, believed in this mirage of the architect as seer and sociological priest. Architecture could reform society, they thought. To match an ideal architecture of steel and glass, based on prefabrication and functional clarity, a new type of person would arise — Le Corbusier's Modulor figures, as it were, in flesh and blood: a lover of speed and socialism, plain food, fresh paint, hygiene, sun-baths, low ceilings, and soccer.[13]

Hughes writes further that "the ideal of social transformation through architecture and design was one of the driving forces of modernist culture. Rational design would make rational societies."[14]

Philip Johnson who, along with Henry Russell Hitchcock, helped popularize the modern movement in the United States through the exhibition and book *The International Style*, recalls:

It was one of those illusions of the 20s, we were thoroughly of the opinion that if you had good architecture the lives of people would be improved; that architecture would improve people, and people improve architecture until perfectibility would descend on us like the Holy Ghost, and we would be happy for ever after. This did not prove to be the case.[15]

In his book *From Bauhaus to Our House* Tom Wolfe asks the obvious question of one of Le Corbusier's worker housing projects in Pessac, France:

And how did the workers like worker housing? Oh, they complained, which was their nature at this stage of history. At Pessac the poor creatures were frantically turning Corbu's cool cubes inside out trying to make them cozy and colorful. But it was understandable. As Corbu himself said, they had to be "reeducated" to comprehend the beauty of "the Radiant City" of the future. In matters of taste, the architects acted as the workers' cultural benefactors. There was no use consulting them directly, since, as Gropius had pointed out, they were as yet "intellectually underdeveloped".[16]

One need not accept clever critics' interpretations of modern architects' attitudes toward the publics they were supposedly serving; the architects made their opinions of people, real people, quite clear. Le Corbusier, for example, said, "Men are so stupid that I'm glad I'm going to die."[17] On a similar tack, another of the triumvirate of "masters of the modern movement" Mies van der Rohe, Philip Johnson's one-time boss, wrote in his 1924 essay "Architecture and the Times":

We are concerned today with questions of a general nature. *The individual is losing significance; his destiny is no longer what interests us* [my italics]. The decisive achievements in all fields are impersonal and their authors for the most part unknown. They are part of the trend of our time toward anonymity. Our engineering structures are examples. Gigantic dams, great industrial installations and huge bridges are built as a matter of course, with no designer's name attached to them. They point to the technology of the future.[18]

Though not as vociferous in his rhetoric as the Europeans, America's master of modern architecture Frank Lloyd Wright regularly differentiated between "Genius" (himself) and "The Mobocracy" (apparently everyone else).[19]

John Thackara summarizes present-day opinions of the modern movement, saying, "There are two popular prejudices about modernist practice: first, that it treats all places and all people in the same way, an approach perceived to be a threat to individual identity and local tradition; and second, that it elevates expert judgment over everyday experience and learned, tacit knowledge."[20] Viewed now, in terms of the extensive criticism of modernism and the range of opposition movements that have now developed, Pevsner's claim that modern architecture constitutes *the* genuine, universal style seems grossly overstated. Modernism as a style for the most part has passed, just like the fashions it was to have replaced. We can hope too that Pevsner was also wrong in assuring us that the "warmth and directness . . . of craft" and the "more personal relationship between architect and client" are passing fashions. We can hope, instead, that these qualities become the universal aspects of design practice.

There are still many defenders of modernism, however, including Ada Louise Huxtable, who wrote in 1981:

There are no more dramatic changes than those that have taken place in the 20th century built environment. We have watched modern cities explode and seen their skylines remade as they have turned into incredible displays of glass and steel and concrete, unlike anything ever know before. Only the names remain the same. None of this could have been constructed, in engineering or technological terms alone, in any other century and the modern architecture of the cityscape has become the universal 20th-century style.[21]

She tellingly goes on to say, "It does not matter whether anyone likes it or not."[22] Here in a nutshell we have all of the modern prejudices, as set out by Pevsner: architecture is to be driven by technology, not human needs; the result is modernism — the *inevitable*, universal twentieth-century style. Aside from anything else, Huxtable's assertion is untrue. There has recently been a proliferation of antimodern styles. The advocates of these new styles reject, to varying degrees, the canons of the "universal style," which then, by definition, is no longer universal.

Huxtable writes further:

Perhaps if modern architecture's stated ambitions had been less large, it would have been less vulnerable. But those ambitions were part of a period of tremendous optimism about the pefectability of man and his social and political systems and the conditions of his life [but, to paraphrase Huxtable, it does not matter whether man wanted to be perfected by modern architecture or not]. The early years of this century were full of courage and hope. Now we are coming to terms with reality and despair.[23]

The reality we are coming to terms with is that of cities scarred by the work of modern architects and it is the attendant despair that has led to the many reactions against modern architecture.

The "New Epoch" of which Le Corbusier wrote and that Huxtable praises is now the old one. The basic premises of the modern movement have been demonstrated to be unworkable at worst and undesirable at best. The attempt to standardize people, making us secondary cogs in a larger societal machine whose metaphor was the factory has failed, as has the attempt to reform, improve, and reeducate people to these "higher goals" through manipulation of built form. The rejection of the universal and unitary design advocated by the modernists was perhaps more inevitable than any aspect of modernist practice and was signaled by the publication of Robert Venturi's 1966 book *Complexity and Contradiction in Architecture*. Venturi outlined an approach to architecture that, in contradistinction to modern architecture, was nonstraightforward, ambiguous, and antiuniversal. This formulation is commonly considered to be the beginning of postmodern architecture, the first comprehensive challenge to the approach of the modern architects.

POSTMODERNISM

Postmodernism in architecture, as set out by Robert Venturi, was a direct challenge to many of the premises upon which modern architecture was based. Charles Jencks, one of the first critics to champion the approach, says in defining postmodernism:

The architect can no longer assume an identity of tastes and goals. There is an inevitable disjunction between the elites who create the environment and the various publics that inhabit and use it. Post-Modern Architecture has grown in power to overcome this disjunction. Or perhaps, more accurately, the major motive of Post-Modern architects is to deal with this disjunction. Whether they are altogether successful at double-coding, at reaching the profession *and* the public is another question. But this leads to the definition: *Post-Modern Architecture is doubly-coded, half-Modern and half-conventional, in its attempt to communicate with both the public and a concerned minority, usually architects.*[24]

Postmodern architects do not change the way in which they work, principally through the use of scale drawings, nor do they change their relationship with clients and users; these are as they were in modernism. Postmodern architects do, however, as Jencks' quote reveals, acknowledge the "taste codes" of the public as a source for inclusion in their compositions in the belief that this will help their work communicate with the users of architecture.

In his first book, *Complexity and Contradiction in Architecture*, Venturi focused on the quality of postmodern space, which he defined in opposition to the simplified, rationalized, and "universal" space in modern architecture:

Architects can no longer afford to be intimidated by the puritanically moral language of orthodox Modern architecture. I like elements which are hybrid rather than "pure," compromising rather than "clean," distorted rather than "straightforward," ambiguous rather than "articulated," perverse as well as impersonal, boring as well as "interesting," conventional rather than "designed," accommodating rather than excluding, redundant rather than simple, vestigial as well as innovating, inconsistent and equivocal rather than direct and clear. I am for messy vitality over obvious unity. I include the non sequitur and proclaim the duality. . . .

I am for richness of meaning rather than clarity of meaning; for the implicit function as well as the explicit function. I prefer "both-and" to "either-or,' black and white, and sometimes gray, to black and white. A valid architecture evokes many levels of meaning and combinations for focus: its space and its elements become readable and workable in several ways at once. But an architecture of complexity and contradiction has a special obligation toward the whole: its truth must be in its totality or its implications of totality. It must embody the difficult unity of inclusion rather than the easy unity of exclusion. More is not less.[25]

Venturi's philosophy of design is encompassed in a series of aphorisms that are set up in opposition to modernist beliefs. "More is not less," for example, is in contrast to Mies van der Rohe's statement, "Less is more."

In his book Venturi introduced another of the central themes of postmodernism — the role of symbolism in architecture, which had been a taboo topic for the moderns. Venturi's views were more heretical still because he acknowledged that there was value, as a source of formal invention, in "honky-tonk elements," those environmental interventions made by nondesigners:

The main justification for honky-tonk elements in architectural order is their very existence. They are what we have. Architects can bemoan or try to ignore them or even try to abolish them, but they will not go away. Or they will not go away for a long time, because architects do not have the power to replace them (nor do they know what to replace them with), and because these commonplace elements accommodate existing needs for variety and communication. The old clichés involving both banality and mess will still be the context of our new architecture, and our new architecture significantly will be the context for them. I am taking the limited view, I admit, but the limited view, which architects have tended to belittle, is as important as the visionary view, which they have tended to glorify but have not brought about. The short-term plan, which expediently combines the old and the new, must accompany the long-term plan. Architecture is evolutionary as well as revolutionary. As an art it will acknowledge what is and what ought to be, the immediate and the speculative. . . .

In God's Own Junkyard Peter Blake has compared the chaos of commercial Main Street with the orderliness of the University of Virginia. Besides the irrelevancy of the comparison, is not Main Street almost all right? Indeed, is not the commercial strip of a Route 66 almost all right? As I have said, our question is: what slight twist of context will make them all right?[26]

**Robert Venturi.
The Duck and the
Decorated Shed.**
Venturi's diagram illustrating the nature of the "plural coding" that is central to postmodern architecture.

Venturi's belief in the value of popular symbolism is further developed in the book *Learning from Las Vegas*, which he wrote with his partners Denise Scott Brown and Steven Izenour. The book documents the results of an architectural studio conducted by the authors with students from Yale University, who studied the Las Vegas strip and attempted to come to terms with the iconography of symbols found there as sources for architectural design. One of Venturi's central ideas, introduced in yet another aphorism, is the opposition between buildings as "ducks" and buildings as "decorated sheds." Ducks, according to Venturi, are buildings whose shape expresses their purpose — the nature of the building as a building. Examples of ducks would be a hot-dog-shaped hot-dog stand or a modern building whose "structural purity" is its sole symbolic content. On the other hand, a decorated shed is a building with two aspects — a functional shed with applied decoration as an explicit symbol. The casinos in Las Vegas, with their elaborate light displays, are examples of decorated sheds. Venturi and his coauthors write:

Why do we uphold the symbolism of the ordinary via the decorated shed over the symbolism of the heroic via the sculptural duck? Because this is not the time and ours is not the environment for heroic communication through pure architecture. Each medium has its day, and the rhetorical environmental statements of our time — civic, commercial, or residential — will come from media more purely symbolic, perhaps less static and more adaptable to the scale of our environment. The iconography and mixed media of roadside commercial architecture will point the way, if we look.[27]

As indicated in the preceding statement they advocate an architecture that is "ugly and ordinary," as represented by the postmodern decorated shed, over "heroic and original" architecture, such as the ducks of the modern movement.

The rationale behind Venturi and his collaborators' view is that

Many people like suburbia. This is the compelling reason for learning from Levittown. The ultimate irony is that although Modern architecture from the start has claimed a strong social basis for its philosophy, Modern architects have worked to keep formal and social concerns separate rather than together. In dismissing Levittown, Modern archi-

**Philip Johnson.
Glass House,
New Canaan,
Connecticut, 1949.**
A "duck" by Philip
Johnson. Here the sole
symbolic content is the
"structural purity" of his
use of modern materials
— steel and glass.

tects, who have characteristically promoted the role of the social sciences in architecture, reject whole sets of dominant social patterns because they do not like the architectural consequences of these patterns. Conversely, by defining Levittown as "silent-white-majority" architecture, they reject it again because they do not like what they believe to be the silent white majority's political views. These architects reject the very heterogeneity of our society that makes the social sciences relevant to architecture in the first place. As Experts with Ideals, who pay lip service to the social sciences, they build for Man rather than for men — this means, to suit themselves, that is, to suit their own particular upper-middle-class values, which they assign to all mankind. Most suburbanites reject the limited formal vocabularies architects' values promote, or accept them 20 years later modified by the tract builder: The Usonian house becomes the ranch house. Only the very poor, via public housing, are dominated by architects' values. Developers build for markets rather than for Man and probably do less harm than authoritarian architects would do if they had the developers' power.[28]

One of the chief strengths of postmodernism seems to be its pluralism — its opposition to the universal and unitary philosophy of modern architecture. As British design theorist John Chris Jones writes:

Suddenly, in architecture and the arts, the modern age (the time of progress, functionalism, abstraction, etc.) is over. Instead we have a new nostalgia, a revival of the past, even of the recent modernist past. At first sight this seems like a loss of nerve, a flight from the present. But, behind the apparent weakness, jokeyness, of post-modernist fashions, is, I think, a new wisdom, hitherto absent from the thought of our time: the notion that progress, and "the new", need no longer *replace* the old. What exists is good, in its own way; there is no need to destroy it. The new and the old can exist together, side-by-side.[29]

The major weakness of postmodernism is that it does not go far enough in its acknowledgment of the wishes of users; it does not actually address the faults implicit in modernist architectural practice, but rather tacitly accepts them. While Venturi berated, tested, prodded, and inverted the philosophy of modern architecture he did not actually deviate from the canons of modern architecture in which he was trained. He acknowledged the *symbolic value* of popular taste

**Philip Johnson
and John Burgee.
AT&T Corporate
Headquarters,
New York, 1983.**
"A decorated shed" by
Johnson's firm. The
modern skyscraper
"shed" is decorated
with pink granite and
a Chippendale top.

codes not for their own value, but only as fodder for the architect's formal compositions. Having completed this formal transformation, Venturi's work has no more actual relevance to the "man in the street" whose taste codes he has adopted than the pop art paintings of Jasper Johns or Andy Warhol, which he cites, have to do with the meaning (as opposed to the form) of the American flags or the Campbell's soup cans they painted. Venturi is very clear on this — his is not a populist vision of architecture, but rather an elitism based on different symbols:

Finally, learning from popular culture does not remove the architect from his status in high culture. But it may alter high culture to make it more sympathetic to current needs and issues. Since high culture and its cultists (last year's variety) are powerful in urban renewal and other establishment circles, we feel that people's architecture as the people want it (and not as some architect decides Man needs it) does not stand much chance against urban renewal until it hangs in the academy and therefore is acceptable to the decision makers. Helping this to happen is a not-reprehensible part of the role of the high-design architect; it provides, together with moral subversion through irony and the use of a joke to get to seriousness, the weapons of the artist of nonauthoritarian temperament in a social situation that does not agree with him. The architect becomes a jester.[30]

In interpreting Venturi's position Tom Wolfe noted:

Not for a moment did Venturi dispute the underlying assumptions of modern architecture: namely, that it was to be for *the people*; that it should be *non-bourgeois* and have *no applied decoration*; that there was a *historical inevitability* to the forms that should be used;

**Venturi and Rauch.
Tucker House,
Katonah, New York,1975.
Exterior view.**
In this design Venturi's
firm's guiding metaphor
for decorating the shed
was the form of a house
when drawn by children.

and that the architect, from his vantage point inside the compound, would decide what was best for the people and what they inevitably should have. . . .

As for the people, the middle-middle class, Venturi regarded them in precisely the same way that the Silver Prince [Walter Gropius] had regarded the proles of fifty years before. They were intellectually underdeveloped, although Venturi was never so gauche as to use such terms. One did not waste time asking them what they liked. As was customary within the compounds, the architect made decisions in this area.[31]

The arbitrary, occasionally inappropriate, and sometimes downright insulting character that Venturi's use of popular symbolism as an architectural device can have is perhaps best illustrated by the case of one of Venturi's firm's earliest works, the Guild House, a Quaker home for the elderly in Philadelphia that was completed in 1963. Venturi placed an oversized, nonfunctioning, gold anodized TV antenna on top of the building as a "symbol" of the elderly who were housed there. Of this decision Venturi says, "The television antenna . . . express-

**Venturi and Rauch.
Tucker House,
Katonah, New York, 1975.
Interior view.**
The exterior house form
is also reflected on the
interior at the hearth,
the symbolic center of
the house.

es a kind of monumentality . . . with its anodized gold surface, [it] can be interpreted in two ways: abstractly, as a sculpture in the manner of Lippold, and as
a symbol for the aged, who spend so much time looking at T.V."[32] The residents
were not consulted about Venturi's choice of a symbol but demanded that the
antenna, which they found demeaning, be removed. Charles Jencks rightly
points out that one of the dangers of postmodern architecture is that of, "adopting plural coding without degenerating into compromise and unintended pas-
tiche."[33] In this case the architect was, as Venturi prescribed, a jester, but the
joke was on the elderly residents of his building. They were not amused.

   The philosophy of postmodernism acknowledged users and their "taste
codes" but the focus of the architectural design process — architecture as formal art object — remained unchanged. Postmodernism, while a challenge to
modernism, takes place firmly *within* the academy; the canons of architectural
practice are not themselves questioned, nor are its processes or methods. Post-
modern architecture results instead in a merely superficial change in the
appearance of buildings. While laypeople may (or may not) like the appearance
of postmodern architecture — with its recollection of styles of the past — better
than that of modern architecture, the needs and wishes of design users are no
better accounted for in one than in the other. In the foreword to Venturi's *Complexity and Contradiction in Architecture*, Vincent Scully writes, "The essential
point is that Venturi's philosophy and design are humanistic . . . it values above
all else the actions of human beings and the effect of physical form upon their
spirit."[34] But, as we have seen, Venturi, the archetypal practitioner of postmodern architecture, has not fundamentally challenged the modernist design pro-

cess itself and is not, therefore, any more successful than modern architects such as Le Corbusier in realizing these elevated goals. With postmodernism, style through symbolism is mistaken for substance through design.

LATE MODERNISM AND DECONSTRUCTION

Postmodernism was not embraced by all architects. Some saw the use of the architectural forms of the past as a reactionary flight from the present. One such architect is Peter Eisenman, who wrote, in the opaque prose for which he is known:

This burying of modern architecture by "post-modern" savants . . . in order to resurrect their loose mixture of historicism and eclecticism, this renunciation of the alleged elitism of rational imagery in favor of an operation that in fact has as one of its objectives not only the elimination of the particular critical ideology of modernism but the elimination of ideology in general from architecture suggests that it is not so much the forms of modernism, the particular social, political or aesthetic ideology its practitioners espoused, but more the fact that the forms contained an ideology at all that is at the core of the "post-modern" reaction.[35]

Some of those architects who rejected postmodernism sought to develop further the ideologies, as they perceived them, of the modern movement. Two of these approaches are late modernism, which extends the formal invention common to modernism, and deconstruction, which attempts to respond to the nature of "true" modernism, as present in the other arts. Though late modernism and deconstruction are rather different trends they can be examined through the work of Peter Eisenman who has practiced both styles of architecture.

Late modernism, as defined by Charles Jencks, "takes the ideas and forms of the Modern Movement to an extreme, exaggerating the structure and technological image of the building in an attempt to provide amusement, or aesthetic pleasure."[36] Late-modern architects adopt the *forms* of modernism while rejecting the social and moral purposes that were the foundation of the movement. This transition is made clear by recalling Suzanne Stephens's comments on Richard Meier's Bronx Development Center, which is designed in the late-modern style: "If the *morality* of Modernism's functionalist credos is no longer the crucial issue, a new kind of morality has sprouted up around architecture's formal and aesthetic obligations."[37] So with late-modern architecture we see a strange shift in emphasis in which architecture is about architecture, having a "moral" obligation only to itself — not to its users.

Extraordinary as it may seem, this is not the isolated point of view of a single critic but rather is the underpinning of the whole of late modernism, a point emphasized by Peter Eisenman: "My first concern in looking at the nature of architecture involved an attempt to change the nature of the sign of the substance — from referring to man to referring to architecture itself."[38] Elsewhere he writes, "What is being proposed is an expansion beyond the limitations presented by the

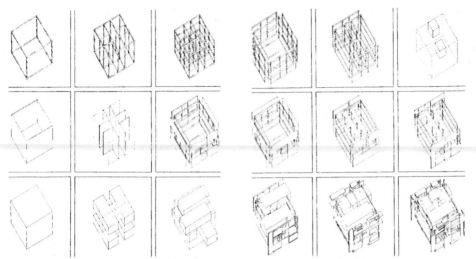

Peter Eisenman. House IV, 1971. Transformational Diagrams. These diagrams, versions of which are used as the basis of all Eisenman's house designs, are part of his attempt "to operate as freely as possible from functional considerations."

classical model to the realization of architecture as an independent discourse, free from external values."[39] In Eisenman's view, presumably, the architect should be free from the consideration of user requirements, as well.

Throughout his work Eisenman is concerned with rejecting what he feels to be the anthropocentric nature of architecture — it is his desire to make architecture not just an art but fine art, truly analogous to contemporary developments in other arts. The critical difference between art and architecture — that one can take or leave the former, but must interact with the latter — is not a concern to Eisenman. His "post-functional" work is intended to "challenge" people's preconceptions about the use of environments.

The most infamous of Eisenman's late modern, "postfunctional" works was House VI for the Franks, built in Cornwall, Connecticut, in 1975. Eisenman says of House VI: "This work is an attempt to transcend our traditional view of: designing, seeing, understanding — our environment. It is an attempt to *alienate* [my italics] the individual from the known way in which he perceives and understands his environment."[40] In reviewing Eisenman's development of a "new metaphysic of dining" in his houses, Roger Kimball writes:

Concerning the [metaphysic of dining], for example, we learn that Houses III and IV explore "an alternative process of making occupiable form . . . a process specifically developed to operate as freely as possible from functional considerations. From a traditional point of view, several columns 'intrude on' and 'disrupt' the living and dining areas as a result of this process. . . . Nonetheless, these dislocations . . . have, according to the occupants of the house, changed the dining experience in a real and, more importantly, unpredictable fashion". Please note that Mr. Eisenman does not assert that the occupants claim that his ill-placed columns have done anything to make "the dining experience" more *pleasant*. Nor would he want them to. For one of the main goals of Mr. Eisenman's architecture (and his writing, too, one suspects) is to subvert anything so bourgeois as comfort or intelligibility. As he puts it, his houses "attempt to have little to do with the traditional and existing metaphysic of the house, the physical and psychological gratification associated with the traditional form of the house . . . in order to initi-

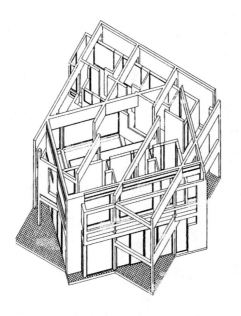

**Peter Eisenman.
House III, 1970.
Axonometric view.**
This drawing represents
the outcome of a series
of geometrical transposi-
tions based on a pair of
rotated squares.

ate a search for those possibilities of dwelling that may have been repressed by that metaphysic"... If Mr. Eisenman can be said to have a thesis, it is the standard academic chestnut that the threat of nuclear weapons, has rendered the traditional notion of home — more, the traditional notion of man — otiose."[41]

Eisenman seems to believe that his deciding that "home" and "man" have become futile concepts gives him a license to do whatever he wants, that he need be responsive to only one constituency — himself. Kimball concludes his analysis by saying:

Eisenman — like so many others these days — pretends that *asserting* something about the aim or meaning of a building is tantamount to *accomplishing* it. But in art, as in life, there is often a great gap between assertion and accomplishment [a fact we will return to

**Peter Eisenman.
House III for
Robert Miller.
Lakeville, Connecticut,
1971. Exterior view.**
A diagram realized in
built form.

23

when examining the "applicability gap" inherent in most design research]. A poorly designed dining room is meant to challenge the conventional "metaphysic of dining," but is really only a poorly designed dining room."[42]

Similar concerns about Eisenman's work are echoed by David Clarke:

Real calamity strikes when you get arted-up *and* intellectual buildings, such as the infamous House VI. . . . Eisenman's intellectual niche has been carefully cultivated to be unlocatable, but Diane Ghirardo, who has worked at locating it, cites "Foucault, Derrida, and poststructuralism" as the main sources. Clever columns are levitated off the ground. A column is a guest that will not go away at the dinner table. The local building inspector insisted on adding two I-beams to keep the house from literally shearing apart. The kitchen is extraordinarily inconvenient in its layout. The wall cabinets are higher than usual, for artistic-intellectual reasons. The clients later had a child — and there was no bedroom for it, and no way to add one on. Since there is no privacy anywhere, there is no way to close any door from the child should it choose to scream all night, which it probably will do after falling off the stairs without a railing. The only bathroom can be arrived at only through the parents' bedroom. "Floorlights" in the bedroom require twin beds, although the parents were used to sleeping together. In a statement to *Newsweek*, Eisenman said that his houses are not shaped for his clients' needs but are "designed to *shake* them out of those needs".[43]

In an interview between Charles Jencks and Peter Eisenman, Jencks questions Eisenman on the house.

Charles Jencks: Your House VI, you know the stairs, and the famous kitchen table are polemically anti-functional and . . .

Peter Eisenman. House VI for the Franks. Cornwall, Connecticut, 1975. Interior view. One of the "post-functional" aspects of this design was the "nowhere stair" that decends, upside-down, in the upper right of the picture.

Peter Eisenman: No, they were against the symbolism of function.

CJ: No, no, they don't work. . . .

PE: People live in them.

CJ: But the hole cut in the bedroom floor and having to add rails on the stairs and having a stairway that doesn't work, all of that was polemically anti-functional — I think it's useless for you to pretend it isn't — you said it, critics said it. You were even proud that your House II was not lived in by the mathematician it was built for, so why the sudden denials?

PE: It is not a denial, I am merely trying to make it clear I was never anti-functional. I believe there is a difference between being anti-functions, and being against making function thematic.

CJ: But there was a part of you which was proud of the fact that that mathematician couldn't live in the house, and often you seem to be against content and against things working.

PE: Again I would argue that the work was certainly not anti-function but against symbolizing function. Those houses keep the rain out, you can sleep in them. . . .

CJ: Yes, but with great difficulty.

PE: No, with different attitudes towards what it means to function as a house. . . . My work attacks the concept of occupation as given. It is against the traditional notion of how you occupy a house.

CJ: Right, and the holes in the floor in the room attack the notion of how you occupy and how you step across the living room?

PE: And having a column in the middle of the bedroom so you could not put a bed in it certainly attacked the notion of how you occupy a bedroom.[44]

Eisenman's current view is that a true modernism has never been achieved in architecture, as it has in the other arts. A central feature of modernism, according to Eisenman, is the alienation of the lone individual and this, not the "universal man" of modernism, or the family from Levittown of postmodernism, seems to be who Eisenman is designing for. He addresses this point in the interview with Jencks: "I am talking about a man who is fulfilling himself through his unconscious, realizing that the emptiness is *in* man and that the alienation lies between the conscious and unconscious individual."[45] Jencks questioned him further:

CJ: So your definition of Modernism as alienation is first of all, as you have already admitted, only really possible outside of architecture, it isn't true *of* architecture.

PE: It has not been true of architecture, but I think it should be. I think it's more difficult in architecture because, as I have said on many occasions, architecture is so rooted in presence and in seeing itself as shelter and institution, house and home. It is the guardian of reality. It is the last bastion of location. I think this is the real problem. Architecture represses dislocation because of the paradoxical position it maintains. You don't have that problem with theology or philosophy or science.[46]

Eisenman is now one of the leaders of the deconstruction, deconstructivist, or deconstructionist movement in architecture (the precise choice of term depends on which critical splinter group one is allied with). This approach is really a development of the antifunctional, antiuser, in fact antipeople, pure architecture-for-architecture's-sake approach implicit in Eisenman's House VI, though now believed to be an expression of "true" modernism in architecture. Roger Kimball gives an overview of the approach:

Deconstructivism . . . this barbarous neologism — which derives from the more familiar term "deconstruction" — denotes a theory and practice of architecture motivated largely by various ideas and catch-phrases appropriated from chic literary theory. One thus sees architects obsessed with language, rejecting traditional aesthetic values like clarity, order, and harmony, and designing buildings that seek to undermine or "deconstruct" such conventional "prejudices" as the desire for comfort, stability, and commodiousness.[47]

Jencks further develops this idea:

For some people nothing has more credibility than the Great Void and the seriousness with which certain New Yorkers pursue this *nihil* would suggest it is located near midtown Manhattan. But, since architecture is supposed to be a constructive art with a social base, an architect who design for emptiness and non-being is slightly humorous. Who's to say? A Deconstructive, anti-social architecture has as great a right to exist as the same traditions in art, literature, and philosophy (as long as one builds it for oneself or a knowing client). . . . Although it may seem absurd to base building on this solipsism and skepticism, architecture always represents general cultural values, and no one will dispute that these are current, even fashionable, motives in the other arts. . . .

Here we touch on a paradox of Deconstruction. . . . This ultra-poetic use of language is virtually private and therefore authoritarian; fully architectural language must, by definition, be more public.[48]

The implications of Eisenman's current views are addressed in an anonymous review of a lecture he delivered at the Architectural Association in London in which he discussed his Cannaregio project. According to the reviewer the project was

A housing scheme for Venice which consisted of a series of totally unusable "houses" set within each other like a Russian doll. Here is architecture as perfect art. The artist/architect has decided that, notwithstanding the wishes of his clients (to build housing for poor people) so many poor people are leaving Venice that housing should not be built at all — only monuments to an architect's ego (which, purged by the horrors of Auschwitz and Hiroshima, must be morally superior to the wishes of staid Venetian bureaucrats).

In a just world, sooner of later Eisenman would get his come-uppance for using this kind of moral blackmail on his audiences and on his clients. But, of course, he will not. Eisenman will go on playing elegant geometrical games for rich clients and justifying them by references to man's inhumanity and to outmoded painters.[49]

The key aspect of late modern and deconstructive architecture seems not to be the formal properties of either, but rather their total disregard of design

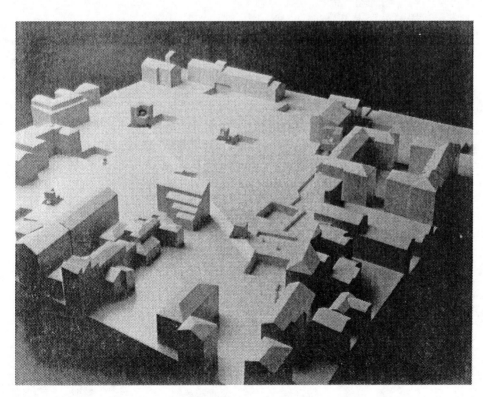

Peter Eisenman. Project for Cannaregio Town Square. Venice, Italy, 1980. In this project Eisenman disagreed with the client's brief, which called for housing for the poor, so he disregarded it, providing instead a design for non-functioning monument.

27

users. They are hermetically sealed approaches to architecture as a fine art whose practitioners believe themselves to be without any social purpose or under any obligation to the public. It hardly seems necessary in the case of late modernism and deconstruction to pose this rhetorical question: To what extent do they respond to the needs and wishes of design users? The modernists aimed to have a moral and social purpose, but failed to realize their goal of perfecting man. Postmodernists were more modest in their aims, adopting familiar symbolism in an attempt to make their work better understood by the public. The late modern and deconstructive architects, however, are practicing an explicitly amoral and antisocial architecture. Perhaps this type of architecture does in some sense reflect our time. Perhaps it is the logical outcome of a design profession that has become more and more insulated from the constituencies it is to serve. Whatever the reasons for the development of this type of architecture, it is essentially an elaborate dead end that is responsive only to the needs of a small group of aesthetes.

THE SECOND MODERNITY

In the previous sections I have quoted extensively from architects' own accounts of their work in order to demonstrate the chasm that exists between designers' views and those of the people who must live with their designs — a condition common to all design philosophies that have emerged since industrialization. As we have seen, whatever style they champion, designers' primary concern is with the "beautiful" arrangement of geometrical shapes, a static and formal criteria dictated by their use of two-dimensional scale drawings as a design media. In their work architects do not meaningfully consider the dynamic experience of users, of which their methods take no account. This phenomenon is so pervasive that — as has been demonstrated with the Bronx Development Center — many buildings can be judged "architectural" successes based on their form alone, no matter how badly suited they are to the purposes for which they were built.

The responses to the process of industrialization from within the architectural profession have been both inadequate and inappropriate. The moderns adopted the factory as a metaphor for buildings and designers, advocating standardization and mass production as the bases for the building task. The not-so-hidden agenda of the moderns was the perfection of man by architects and through architecture. The opinions of the people to be affected by modern design didn't matter since they had not, as yet, been "reeducated." Modern architecture was to have been a universal style for the elevation of universal man.

The "universal style" despite, or perhaps because of, its lofty and unattainable goals, failed and was superseded, in the four-color press at least, by a range of competing styles. The first reaction against modernism, postmodernism, constituted a rejection of the singly coded "ducks" of the modern age in favor of doubly coded "decorated sheds," which were half-modern to communicate with an educated elite and half conventional, incorporating popular symbolism to communicate with the public. Postmodern architecture essentially consists of a modern building decorated in eclectically chosen styles from the past. Though postmodernists employed popular symbolism, it was used only as raw material for architects' compositions. Postmodernism did not constitute a fundamental challenge to the modernist design process itself, nor was the relationship between designers and users radically reformed by the approach.

Because of the essentially superficial nature of the postmodern reaction to modernism, it in turn was rejected by some architects attempting to refine the ideology of modernism itself. The late modernists, for example, took the formal ideas of the modern movement further, while disregarding the social ideals and moral purposes that led to the foundation of the movement in the first place. The deconstructivists, on the other hand, have sought to develop the concept of modernism as the alienation of the individual more fully in architecture, as it is present in the other arts. One approach to this is the design of "postfunctional" buildings that "alienate" users from their needs and wishes. Both late modernism and deconstruction are self-referential approaches that explicitly seek to make architecture itself, not people, the focus of architectural activity.

The inadequacies of contemporary approaches to design are further highlighted when viewed in terms of the changing nature of design in the postindustrial era. As noted earlier, design in the postindustrial era will have to be more responsive to user concerns than had been the case during the industrial age. In fact postindustrial design will have many of the attributes of preindustrial craftwork: high quality, well adapted to its context of use, customizable, and, in some cases, individualized. A truly postindustrial design would, in other words, be diametrically opposed to the fundamental principles of the modern movement.

The issues that prompted the development of modernism, such as the attempt to humanize industrial life and smooth the relationship of man to machine, are still unresolved. The failure of the modernists to realize the goals they set for themselves is well documented. And, as we have seen, whatever the merits or demerits of the design approaches that have arisen since modernism — including postmodernism, late modernism, and deconstruction — they do not resolve, and in large part they do not even attempt to resolve, the fundamental questions posed by the modernists. Venturi and his coauthors themselves admit: "Since we have criticized Modern architecture, it is proper here to state our intense admiration of its early period when its founders, sensitive to their own times, proclaimed the right revolution. Our argument lies mainly with the irrelevant and distorted prolongation of that old revolution today."[50]

But this begs the question of what is the appropriate revolution for design today. With so many questions of a fundamental nature left outstanding, can the postmodern retreat into symbolism alone be the answer? No, say the late modernists and deconstructivists. But then one must ask whether the adoption of an amoral formalism is the solution either. Again the answer must be no. Yet these are all the choices we have been given by the architectural profession — and all have proven inadequate. What must be concluded from all this is that the architectural profession *doesn't have an answer!* It is becoming apparent that the architectural profession, no matter what it does, does not know how to respond adequately to industrialization and its aftermath. A range of observers of architecture are now suggesting that the field may be bankrupt, the profession itself impotent, and the methods inapplicable to contemporary design tasks. It is further suggested that collectively they are incapable of producing pleasant, livable, and humane environments, except perhaps occasionally and then only by chance.

According to Andrea Branzi we have now entered the "Second Modernity" in which the issues of modernism resurface, but are addressed in new ways. Questioning the usefulness of traditional architectural culture in application to present conditions he writes:

Architectural culture in Europe has been concerned primarily with defending architecture as such, thereby rendering it impervious to innovation. This is due to the mistaken belief that architecture represents an institutional asset that must not be brought into question. . . .

At this moment, European architecture has nothing of real interest to offer, whether in technical, urban, or human terms. It has faced the crisis in classic modernity some ten years later than design, and it has done so in the wrong way. The postmodern movement, in fact, thought that it would be able to handle the crisis it faced by modifying its formal languages, by forcing the physical presence of architecture onto the city, and by seeking to define this discipline as the most mature product of history, without apprehending the necessity and the opportunity for a more sweeping process of self examination. European culture has failed to understand that the increasingly superfluous character of architecture in the metropolis was not the consequence of a momentary crisis but the outcome of a complex shift in the lines along which reality takes shape. It has not grasped that the deterioration of its linguistic heritage could not be halted by drawing indiscriminately on historical codes but that it had to deal with the new codes of current social structure, codes that are perhaps less lofty but certainly more vital. Equally it has not understood that its appeal to history placed it outside the framework of history itself and in conflict with the technology, symbols, patterns of behavior, and dreams of the present day. Refusing to look at the world, it has shut itself up within the universities, turning into an academic discipline based entirely on the power of education, that is to say, on self-reproduction.[51]

Branzi highlights the rather specific ways in which the nature of the design process was changed with the advent of industrialization:

Let us not forget that the very birth of the neoplastic code at the beginning of the century, perhaps representing Classic Modernity more completely than anything else, based its legitimacy on reference to a principle of necessity; that is, from the supposedly indispensable, semantic reduction of reality into simple geometric shapes (spheres, cylinders, straight lines and planes), making it possible for this reality to fit into the machine, to be mass-produced.[52]

This reduction of the design task into the arrangement of simple geometric forms in isolation from the processes of making and the context of use has logically, if regrettably, resulted in design becoming a game played for the architect's amusement, without reference to the experience of design users. Branzi makes a very apt analogy that clarifies the nature of the formal ploys of architects:

Many architects do not realize that, just when they think they are really making architecture, they are in fact playing a game of chess with themselves. That is, they are inventing problems and then solving them brilliantly. Since the game of chess is a difficult one that requires intelligence, they feel their efforts have significance away from the chessboard as well. . . .

In point of fact architecture today has become a pure, gratuitous art, which should be left in the hands of great artists and not professors. It is no longer concerned with the solution of problems of construction but emits pure energy of urban communication, pure domestic imagination. It is not clear why this should be regarded as a tragedy.[53]

To say, as Branzi does, that architecture is becoming a pure, gratuitous art is not simply a metaphor but a reality. Increasingly developers — who, despite any other faults they may have, are compelled to be somewhat responsive to their clients' wishes — are dominating the bulk of building activity. Further, "high-design" architects, such as those we have been discussing, seem to be building fewer and fewer buildings in recent years. It is not uncommon for "famous" architects to have built nothing during the first decade or so of their notoriety. Instead the glossy journals, the university lecture circuit, and, increasingly, art galleries provide the real context for their architectural work. As David Clarke writes, "Architecture today is standing on its head. . . . The four-color press counts for everything; most clients and the general public for nothing."[54]

Like Branzi, however, I do not see that this development constitutes a "crisis in architecture" or a "tragedy." Rather, it represents the realization that high-design architecture is becoming a gallery art. So much the better if galleries such as New York's Max Protetch display recent architectural design on their walls; it is almost certainly better than those same designs being built. Perhaps the patronage of galleries will stop the current antisocial trends in architecture from reproducing and infecting building production as a whole.

The irrelevant and gratuitous nature of present trends in architecture is also addressed by Christopher Alexander, himself a licensed architect and contractor. In response to an editorial by *Progressive Architecture's* executive editor, Thomas Fisher, which denounced Prince Charles' views on architecture, Alexander wrote:

I am appalled by the narrow-minded and ignorant attempt . . . to dismiss Prince Charles and his message. I think the time has come to take the gloves off, and to acknowledge publicly that the cabalistic confraternity of architects in the United States, as in England, has been perpetrating a gigantic scam on the almost unsuspecting public for about 50 years. Few people genuinely like what architects do today or what they have done in the last decades. Yet many people go along for the ride because they are afraid of being thought to have "bad taste" or afraid to seem ignorant of the niceties of "Architecture" with a capital A. . . . Like the sinister tailors in *The Emperor's New Clothes*, they use the ordinary person's fear of seeming ignorant as a weapon to maintain a monopoly on the profession's status quo. Above all, they use it to keep a secure hold on money.

The Executive Editor of *Progressive Architecture* tries to continue the work of the tailors in *The Emperor's New Clothes* by trying to perpetuate the unspoken esoteric knowledge, making it look like sense when it is really nonsense. For example, in his editorial he says Sandy Wilson is bad, James Stirling is good, thus trying to show that there are subtle distinctions of good and bad for those in the know, and thus stifling, or trying to stifle the thought (Oh perish the terrible thought) that there might be something so fundamentally wrong in all of Modern architecture that it is, almost all of it, flawed and misdirected. Yet in fact, from the point of view of real common sense, both works — Wilson's and Stirling's — are merely silly exercises in the same image-ridden nonsense, which we have been pretending for years makes sense.

It just does NOT make sense. Mr. Fisher's attempt to put down Prince Charles is the same tactic that architecture professors use continually in schools of architecture to subdue beginning students by creating a subtle and highly repressive atmosphere of esoteric knowledge. He tries to establish the mysterious existence of a clue of those inner circle architects who are "in the know" — hoping that the vanity of others and their desire to be members of this club will quieten their common sense and muffle the criticism they feel in their hearts.

It is time to stop. It is time to declare that the architects who lay this appalling nonsense on the public are in fact just spouting nonsensical rubbish. It is time to stop the process of intimidating members of the public with architectural faddism. It is time finally to say: LOOK, THE ARCHITECT HAS NO CLOTHES.[55]

Though addressing modern architecture explicitly, Alexander includes postmodernism in his critique as well. Elsewhere he writes, "The games of the Post Moderns are in my mind nothing but intellectualism which have little to do with the core of architecture."[56]

The natural result of all of this public dissatisfaction is that architecture becomes less and less important as clients choose contractors who will listen to them, in preference to architects who will not. And as Robert Venturi and his coauthors point out, contractors will probably do a better job than architects would have done, given the same power.[57] Though architects may not have noticed from the elevated and isolated towers they have constructed for themselves, the architectural profession is becoming an irrelevant, academic discipline. Robert Venturi is almost all right when he writes:

Architects and planners who peevishly denounce the conventional townscape for its vulgarity or banality promote elaborate methods for abolishing or disguising honky-tonk elements in the existing landscape, or, for excluding them from the vocabulary of their new townscapes. But they largely fail either to enhance or to provide a substitute for the existing scene because they attempt the impossible. By attempting too much they flaunt their impotence and risk their continuing influence as supposed experts.[58]

Similarly David Clarke writes:

Why do architects, in a spasm of self-destruction, insist on attempting to make architecture more important than anyone except themselves wants it to be? Because their self-importance is clearly against the general public's interest and desire, they have succeeded in achieving the opposite of their goal: irrelevance. Thus we have an odd conundrum: architects could be much more important in society if they would only try to be less important.[59]

Architecture, in all of its various "isms," has failed during the past century to address adequately the question of living in an industrial, or for that matter postindustrial, age. Comparing contemporary developments to the concerns of William Morris, Branzi writes:

At the Red House, William Morris was looking for the nucleus of a new way of living. His proposal was neo-medieval, one in which the craftsman's workshop was the center of a different sort of society, and manual technique the way of achieving a renewed domestic civilization. The excessive development of architectural research certainly has not resolved, and actually has hardly dealt with, the problem of a new way of living, to the extent that all modern architecture has developed without any real awareness of how it is to be used. No wonder it has now reached a point of advanced social isolation.[60]

As Branzi rightly points out, the architectural profession has reached a point of "advanced social isolation" owing largely to the fact that architecture since industrialization has developed without regard for the actual users of design. The task, as the modern architects recognized, is to design for a new way of life, but their theories, and those of their successors, have proven inadequate and impotent in application to this task. We must look outside the architectural profession if we wish to discover approaches to design that acknowledge and respond effectively to the needs and wishes of design users.

2. Design Research

The inadequacies of the design professions have become increasingly obvious over the past three decades and a range of disparate approaches has developed in an attempt to make designing more responsive to design users. These approaches include man-environment relations, environment-behavior studies, environmental psychology, and design methods and its offshoots. Collectively these approaches may be termed "design research."

Design research has, for the most part, been conducted outside the traditional design professions by people more concerned with the effects of designing than with its forms. Social scientists, particularly psychologists, sociologists, and anthropologists, have been among those most prevalent in the field of design research; few professional designers have had the time, training, or inclination to pursue it.

Design research developed in response to the perceived failure of the design professions to produce satisfactory environments. The success of design research can be judged by determining the extent to which design has improved since the inception of the field over two decades ago. To what extent has design research led to more satisfactory environments? And at a more structural level, to what extent do the efforts of design researchers constitute meaningful interventions in the design process that positively affect the responsiveness of design to its users?

Viewed more broadly, design research should be concerned with the type of issues William Morris was pursuing at Red House — the seeking of new ways of life. Rather than seeking ways of coping with industrialization, like Morris, however, present-day design research should constitute an experiment to determine how we wish to live in a postindustrial era, as opposed to the way we were compelled to live in the industrial age.

ENVIRONMENT-BEHAVIOR STUDIES

Environment-behavior studies focus principally on the application of methods from the social sciences to an analysis of the quality of the built environment. The most commonly used environment-behavior research techniques are interviews, questionnaires, and laboratory experiments. In general researchers in environment-behavior studies are not practicing designers but hope that designers will will incorporate their research results into their designs.

One of the environment-behavior researchers' central premises is that a wide range of available research data on people's behavior is not being utilized by designers, whose methods focus almost exclusively, as we have seen, on the manipulation of geometrical shapes via drawings. The belief, at least initially, was that like the public in the modern era, designers could be "reeducated" by the environment-behavior researchers about the human requirements for buildings. It was further believed that the architects would embrace this knowledge, apply it directly, and the built environment would consequently improve dramatically. Like the modernists, environment-behavior researchers believed that this would happen *inevitably* — mass production and standardization in this case being replaced by experiments and data as the foundations for a new, improved, and again *improving* design. The positivistic myth of the early environment-behavior researchers was, however, no more sustainable than the similar myths of the moderns.

One of the chief problems with environment-behavior studies has been the conflict between the nature of the research and design tasks themselves. Social-science research is analytical, it generates data pertaining to general cases, whereas the designer, if at all interested in research, needs to create a synthesis in a particular case. The two approaches are antithetical and many designers who were predisposed to the idea of improving their design through application of research results quickly became disillusioned and returned to their previous, formally based methods.

In the literature of the environment-behavior field the reader is told of the *need* for psychology, or sociology, or whatever, in application to architecture. But the need is not for these disciplines per se, but rather to make design more responsive to the needs and wishes of design users. Do the social science disciplines do this? Not directly — they might be able to *inform* the design process but they are not actually part of it. And as Roger Kimball pointed out with regard to the deconstructivists, *asserting* something is not the same as *accomplishing* it, though the two are systematically confused by environment-behavior researchers.

One of the most talked about issues in environment-behavior studies, once the initial enthusiasm for the social sciences waned, has been the "applicability gap" — the failure of most environment-behavior research to be used by designers. The widespread acknowledgment of the applicability gap by environment-behavior researchers is itself a tacit admission that their work is not design at all but an ineffectual commentary on design. In fact one of the most successful environment-behavior techniques is the awkwardly named Post-Occupancy Evaluation, an elaborate survey technique conducted after a building has been used to determine how well the building suits the purposes for which it was intended. Post-occupancy evaluations can usefully identify problems with buildings, but designers require methods that will help them *anticipate* the effects the designs will have. Evaluative techniques such as this are really just cases of the use of common sense and twenty/twenty hindsight; they do not change the nature of the design process itself.

The principal organization devoted to environment-behavior studies is the Environmental Design Research Association (EDRA), founded in 1969. In introducing the first conference proceedings of the organization, co-organizers Henry Sanoff and Sidney Cohn wrote of the nature of environment-behavior research at that time:

In any new area of scientific research and particularly multi-disciplinary scientific investigation, the researchers are plagued with a variety of theoretical, methodological, and even philosophical problems, and errors will be made. . . . The products of these recent investigations into environmental design and behavior tends [sic] to be highly piecemeal in nature. The bits and pieces which indicate promise are not systematically or theoretically related and coordinated; each tends to exist as an entity in and of itself. . . . In some cases the area of research is well formulated, but the research design is poor; in other cases, the research design is well conceived but the conceptualization of the phenomenon lacks relevance to solving the real world problems. Unfortunately the "poor" research tends to further limit the heuristic value of the work.[1]

Over the two decades of its existence EDRA has, if anything, become *less* relevant to design. The positivistic theme of the twenty-first EDRA conference was "Coming of Age." But one of the keynote speakers, Robert Sommer, a leading environment-behavior researcher, admits:

Techniques for bringing design research to the attention of practitioners and space managers include (1) reports describing research findings, (2) articles in trade periodicals, (3) direct consultation on design projects, and (4) legal testimony. None of these methods is likely to provide researchers with feedback on research impact.[2]

Sommer's comments further emphasize the remoteness of environment-behavior research from the actual design task.

Environment-behavior studies began as a revolution, but now where the researchers have any impact at all it is as collaborators in the very design process they set out to reform. Environment-behavior research is, for the most part, neither purely "pure" nor effectively "applied." Instead it consists of academic exercises with no relevance to the design process at all. More importantly, environment-behavior researchers have failed to realize their goal of improving the quality of the built environment. Design today is no more responsive to users than it was when environment-behavior studies was founded. Perhaps the most damning criticism of environment-behavior researchers is simply to note that, despite all of their rhetoric and voluminous publications, the design process has been completely unaffected by their efforts.

The proper business of design research is to design ways in which user needs and wishes may become the central focus of the design process — not simply to repeat the mistake of the moderns, as environment-behavior researchers do, by substituting statistical representations of abstract users for the theory of the universal man. To paraphrase Wallace Stevens's poem, "Not Ideas about the Thing but the Thing Itself", design research, to be effective, must not consist of ideas about design, as is the case with environment-behavior studies, but rather must *be design itself*.

DESIGN METHODS

For all their faults, designers do design — they have a process that works for them, if for no one else. If design researchers hope to make design more responsive to people then they will have to design structural changes into the design process itself, not passively stand by and complain about unfeeling and uncaring designers. Within design research two major trends can be distinguished: those approaches that *directly* address the process of design and those that do not. As we have seen, environment-behavior studies are examples of the latter, in which researchers for the most part tried to apply social science research results to "inform" the design process. This approach has proven ineffective. However, one approach that directly addressed the process of design was the design-methods movement that first developed in Britain during the early 1960s.

The founders of the design methods movement were interested in developing means of design applicable to the new and larger scale design tasks then emerging for which there was no precedent, such as the design of human interfaces with high-technology equipment. The focus of these design tasks was increasingly on human rather than hardware concerns. Designer's traditional ways of working — individually, principally through intuition, and using two-dimensional scale drawings as a design media — were proving increasingly inappropriate in application to these new design tasks. The design-methods movement was an attempt to develop methods that were applicable to these new tasks and that transcended the limitations of the traditional design process. Specifically, design methods were developed to permit many people to collaborate in the design process, in place of the reliance on a single person's ability to know and effectively synthesize all of the information relevant to a design task. In addition, design methods were intended to allow information arrived at rationally to be systematically incorporated into the design process, instead of depending almost exclusively on the intuition of the individual designer, as had previously been the case. Finally, in order to realize these goals, the protagonists of the design-methods movement attempted to change the nature of the design process itself by replacing the principal design technique of the industrial era — "design-by-drawing" — with other, more abstract, methods that permitted a greater "perceptual span" than was possible with traditional design methods.

The two most influential figures in the design-methods movement, John Chris Jones and Christopher Alexander, are both British, though their work developed independently. Jones co-organized the first conference on design methods in London in 1962. Alexander attended the conference and two years later published his book *Notes on the Synthesis of Form,* which had a great impact on the design debate at the time. In 1970 Jones published the first edition of *Design Methods,* a compendium of thirty-five different design methods that was to become the standard textbook on the subject.

The need for new methods of design was eloquently addressed by Alexander:

Today functional problems are becoming less simple all the time. But designers rarely confess their inability to solve them. Instead, when a designer does not understand a problem clearly enough to find the order it really calls for, he falls back on some arbitrarily chosen formal order. The problem, because of its complexity, remains unsolved.

To match the growing complexity of problems, there is a growing body of information and specialist experience. This information is hard to handle; it is widespread, diffuse, unorganized. Moreover, not only is the quantity of information itself by now beyond the reach of single designers, but the various specialists who retail it are narrow and unfamiliar with the form-makers' peculiar problems, so that it is never clear quite how the designer should best consult them. As a result, although ideally a form should reflect all the known facts relevant to its design, in fact the average designer scans whatever information he happens on, consults a consultant now and then when faced by extra-special difficulties, and introduces this randomly selected information into forms otherwise dreamt up in the artist's studio of his mind. The technical difficulties of grasping all the information needed for the construction of such a form are out of hand — and well beyond the fingers of a single individual.

At the same time that the problems increase in quantity, complexity, and difficulty, they also change faster than before. New materials are developed all the time, social patterns alter quickly, the culture itself is changing faster than it has ever changed before. In the past — even after the intellectual upheaval of the Renaissance — the individual designer would stand to *some* extent upon the shoulders of his predecessors. And although he was expected to make more and more of his own decisions as traditions gradually dissolved, there was always still some body of tradition which made his decisions easier. Now the last shreds of tradition are being torn from him. Since cultural pressures change so fast, any slow development of form becomes impossible. Bewildered, the form-maker stands alone. He has to make clearly conceived forms without the possibility of trial and error over time. He has to be encouraged now to think his task through from the beginning, and to "create" the form he is concerned with, for what once took many generations of gradual development is now attempted by a single individual. But the burden of a thousand years falls heavily on one man's shoulders, and this burden has not yet materially been lightened. The intuitive resolution of contemporary design problems lies beyond a single individual's integrative grasp.[3]

The net result of all this, Alexander notes, is that "the very frequent failure of individual designers to produce well organized forms suggests strongly that there are limits to the individual designer's capacity."[4] For Alexander, however, a "well organized form" is not purely an aesthetic judgment but rather a definition of a condition in which physical form is well suited to the context in which it occurs; i.e., there are no mismatches or "misfits" between the form and the process of use. As he writes: "when we speak of design, the real object of discussion is not the form alone, but the ensemble comprising the form and its context. Good fit is a desired property of this ensemble which relates to some particular division of the ensemble into form and context."[5]

John Chris Jones voiced similar views on the need for new methods of design:

Perhaps the most obvious sign that we need better methods of designing and planning is the existence, in industrial countries, of massive unsolved problems that have been created by the use of man-made things, e.g. traffic congestion, parking problems, road accidents, airport congestion, airport noise, urban decay and chronic shortages of such services as medical treatment, mass education and crime detection.[6]

In analyzing the causes of these mismatches of design and use Jones writes:

What do we see if we take a bird's eye view of our efforts, as engineers, architects, planners and industrial designers, to influence the recent course of human evolution? . . . We see a series of products, services, and buildings that are *well suited* to their markets but *ill suited* to the conditions brought about by their use. Why do these major design errors arise? I suggest that it is because existing methods in engineering design, industrial design, marketing, architecture, urban planning and related areas are *conservative, persuasive* and *rigid*. They oblige us to perpetuate inflexible patterns of activity. Our productions are designed on rigid principles that preclude re-adjustment and adaptation to unforeseen effects. We need methods of designing, planning and testing that are *exploratory, predictive* and *flexible*.[7]

Jones concludes on the basis of his analysis that "neither the professional designer, nor the drawing board upon which the parts of a design can be adjusted relative to each other, are essential to the evolution of complex forms that are well fitted to the circumstances in which they are used."[8] He also remarks, "Rethinking the human or 'software' aspects of the organized man-machine systems that are emerging in these areas, is often a greater design challenge than is the design of the 'hardware' components."[9] A prescient remark, especially viewed in terms of the nature of the emerging postindustrial design tasks.

Jones himself originally became involved in design methods while working as an industrial designer for a manufacturer of large electrical products. He was frustrated with the superficiality of industrial design at the time and had become involved with ergonomics. He set up one of the first labs devoted to the discipline in British industry as a means of designing electrical equipment that better responded to user requirements. When the results of his ergonomic studies of user behavior were not utilized by the firm's engineering designers, Jones studied the design process being used by the engineers. To his surprise — and to theirs — Jones's analysis showed that the engineering-design process was almost purely intuitive and that the designers had no way of incorporating data arrived at rationally early on in their design process when it was most needed. Jones then set to work redesigning the engineers' design process itself in such a way that intuition and rationality could coexist, rather than having one present to the exclusion of the other. This was Jones' first experience with design methods.

I discussed his ideas and work in an extensive series of interviews with Jones. Addressing the origin of his work with design methods Jones said:

I didn't want to get involved with design theory or methods, I just wanted to get the ergonomics work into action. I only did the design methods in order to get the ergonomics accepted, and that was there in order to get the product better. I thought, well the right thing is to understand their design process so we'll do ergonomics on the design process. So I did this ergonomics study of how the designing was done purely with the view of getting the ergonomic information, which was obviously sound and well tested into the engineering decision process at the point where it wouldn't be reject-ed — so the human limitations would come first and the machine limitations would come second, instead of the other way round. In doing that I hit on what's now called design methods, I called it "systematic design methods" originally.[10]

Both Jones and Alexander contrasted the rigidity and unresponsiveness of the then-current design methods with previous craft methods that produced objects much more suited to the contexts in which they were used. Jones contrasts prein-dustrial craftwork with the design-by-drawing approach of the industrial era. His comparison is not based on idle romanticism, but rather was an attempt to dis-cover the structural differences in the processes themselves as a means of under-standing why the results of craftwork are so often more satisfying than the products of the industrial age. About the qualities of craftwork Jones writes, "Farm wagons and carts were not designed at all in our sense of the word. No single person had ever sat down to conceive them as a whole . . . [but] they were what we would call 'good designs'."[11] Jones was heavily influenced in his views by *The Wheelwright's Shop*, a book by George Sturt, one of the few traditional craftsmen explicitly to set out the craft process he followed. Jones cites the two positive aspects of wagon making as specified by Sturt, "the accuracy with which the wagons matched the requirements of users, and the way in which the designs transcended conflicts between these requirements to produce a situation which Sturt calls 'the interaction of parts.'"[12] Jones continues:

It is clear therefore that the tremendous time taken to discover the wagon shapes through centuries of evolution was a most important factor. Herein lie both the weak-ness and the strength of the "design method" used. Long evolution by trial and error, and we may be sure that there were countless failures and disasters, is out of the ques-tion in anything but an extremely stable society. In our own society, requirements and materials are never still and this is probably the greatest obstacle to good design.

[The] absence of fashion, or the need to introduce conscious symbolism of feelings not directly associated with the wagon itself, is the second important condition that we seek. It is this "*un*aesthetic" (or *unconsciously* aesthetic) attitude that allowed the wheelwrights to persist until they discovered those beautiful "invisible lines." It is clear that very many of our domestic products do not have the two most striking qualities described by George Sturt; exact matching to requirements and interaction of parts.[13]

Jones contrasts the rigidity and limitations of the process of design in the industrial era, which he terms design-by-drawing, with the responsiveness of the craft process: "The essential difference between [drawing], the normal method of evolving the shapes of machine-made things, and the earlier method of craft evolution, is that trial-and-error is separated from production by using a scale drawing in place of the product as the medium for experi-ment and change."[14] And he notes that the separation of thinking from mak-ing brought about by the use of drawings has several important effects: it enables production work to be split up, it enables the planning of things that are too big for one craftsman to build, and it enables the rate of production of things to increase.

The scope for using drawings as a means of producing well adapted designs is, however, extremely limited, as Jones notes: "the principle of deciding the form of the whole *before the details have been explored outside the mind of the chief designer* does not work in novel situations for which the necessary experience cannot be contained within the mind of one person."[15] Further, when comparing the processes of craftwork with the possibilities opened up by the use of drawings as a medium for design, he writes:

What strikes me most, about this new freedom to design instead of just evolve, is that it is obtained at such high cost, the loss of the ability to adjust the shape of things to reflect what makes life really human. There arises a profound conflict between the geometric uniformity of what the designers *have* understood and the barbaric ignorance of everything non-visual that the scale drawing *fails to represent*.[16]

In discussing design-by-drawing Jones said:

It's just a grotesque procrustean exercise. It's bound to seem very satisfactory to the designers because they can see this beautiful bird's eye view and they can control it. Provided one's skillful enough with a pencil, it'll do what they want so you get beautiful shapes. And it's bound to seem an imposition to the users. But the users will not be aware that it's miles from what they want, they'll be tricked into accepting the professional values — the geometric beauty as the criteria. . . . I've always been annoyed or irritated, or amused if not annoyed, by the way architects say "it doesn't work" or "it does work" and I can never get them, when I question them, to say what they mean by "work," though I think I vaguely know what they mean. It means visual articulation and getting it to look right, really, and in better architects this produces a wondrous quality which still might disregard some things the people in the building need. There's this over simplifying quality always in architecture. But they try, they cover all the fields in a very engaging way and have a great willingness to combine the aesthetic and technical and all those other contradictions. There's an arrogance that goes with it, which gives beautiful confidence but an unfortunate lack of depth, a lack of willingness to get involved in the detail. I think this comes because it's a gentlemanly pursuit originally, not a necessary craft but a luxury.[17]

The extent to which architecture is a luxury and not a necessary craft is borne out by the fact that architects are estimated to be involved in only three to five percent of all building activity worldwide.[18]

Alexander addresses the contrasting methods of craftwork and design-by-drawing as well, but terms them differently. He speaks of "unselfconscious" processes instead of craftwork and "selfconscious" processes instead of design-by-drawing:

The modern designer relies more and more on his position as an "artist," on catchwords, personal idiom, and intuition — for all these relieve him of some of the burden of decision, and make his cognitive problems manageable. Driven on his own resources, unable to cope with the complicated information he is supposed to organize, he hides his incompetence in a frenzy of artistic individuality. As his capacity to invent clearly conceived, well-fitting forms is exhausted further, the emphasis on intuition and individuality only grows wilder.[19]

Alexander's views have been proven correct by recent developments in architecture, particularly by such movements as deconstruction in which — as seen with Peter Eisenman's Cannaregio project in Venice — the design task is completely disregarded if it is too complex. Instead an individual, artistic "creation" unrelated to client's brief is offered in place of a design solution to a specific task.

Alexander goes on to write of the self-conscious process of design-by-drawing:

Let us remember, however, just what things a designer tries to diagram. Physical concepts like "neighborhood" or "circulation pattern" have no more universal validity than verbal concepts. They are still bound by the conceptual habits of the draftsman. A typical sequence of diagrams which precede an architectural problem will include a circulation diagram, a diagram of acoustics, a diagram of the load-bearing structure, a diagram of sun and wind perhaps, a diagram of the social neighborhoods. I maintain that these diagrams are used only because the principles which define them — acoustics, circulation, weather, neighborhood — happen to be part of current architectural usage, not because they bear a well-understood fundamental relation to any particular problem being investigated. In this fashion the selfconscious individual's grasp of problems is constantly misled. His concepts and categories, besides being arbitrary and unsuitable, are self-perpetuating. Under the influence of concepts, he not only does things from a biased point of view, but sees them biasedly as well. The concepts control his perception of fit and misfit — until in the end he sees nothing but deviations from his conceptual dogmas, and loses not only the urge but even the mental opportunity to frame his problems more appropriately.[20]

And here we find the present condition of the architectural profession, whose members, having found their methods inadequate in application to increasingly complex design tasks, are now taking refuge in their own formal conceptual dogmas. As Alexander foresaw, they have now lost both the desire and the ability to produce designs that are responsive to the real contexts in which they will be used.

In unself-conscious processes, such as craftwork, the media of design and making were unified, the model of the object and the object itself were the same; they could be continuously tested and refined in their contexts of use in order to ensure a good fit of form and use. Drawings, however, are abstract representations that bear no relationship to the context of use. As Alexander writes:

We do not know how to express the criteria for success in terms of any symbolic description of a form. In other words, given a new design, there is often no mechanical way of telling, purely from the drawings which describe it, whether or not it meets its requirements. Either we must put the real thing in the actual world, and see whether it works or not, or we must use our imagination and experience of the world to predict from the drawings whether it will work or not. But there is no general symbolic connection between the requirements and the form's description which provide criteria; and so there is no way of testing the form symbolically. . . .

In present design practice, this critical step, during which the problem is prepared and translated into design, always depends on some kind of intuition. Though design is by nature imaginative and intuitive, and we could easily trust it if the designer's intuition were reliable, as it is it inspires very little confidence.[21]

The large number of designs that have failed the test of use in the quarter century since Alexander wrote his book demonstrates that his is a realistic, not a jaundiced, view of the implications of purely intuitive, self-conscious design.

As we have seen, in contrast to present methods such as design-by-drawing, unself-conscious processes rely on trial-and-error experimentation to evolve, rather than design, objects. Of this Alexander writes: "Trial-and-error design is an admirable method. But it is just real world trial and error which we are trying to replace by a symbolic method, because real trial and error is too expensive and too slow. . . . In the unselfconscious process there is no possibility of misconstruing the situation: nobody makes a picture of the context, so the picture cannot be wrong. But the selfconscious designer works entirely from the picture in his mind, and this picture is almost always wrong."[22] He concludes that in this sense "architecture did actually fail from the very moment of its inception. With the invention of a teachable discipline called 'architecture,' the old process of making form was adulterated and its chances of success destroyed."[23]

Here we return to the idea that architects are incapable of producing well adapted environments. Architecture is a self-conscious process in which drawings are used as symbolic media for design. The use of drawings permits a division of labor to take place, separating, for the first time, designing from making. Among the consequences of the use of drawings is that they increase the potential scale of design tasks and the speed with which designing and building can take place. But these gains are realized at the expense of the meaningful consideration of user requirements and the context in which a design will be used. Craftwork, on the other hand, is very well tailored to the conditions in which it is used. It is an unself-conscious process in which trial and error is used to evolve objects directly in their context of use. But the trial and error through which craft objects are developed is slow, expensive, and largely impervious to innovation. The design methods movement was an attempt to capture the quality of craftwork in the new, larger design tasks that were then emerging. Specifically, the methods were attempts to develop a means for symbolically representing the design task that matched physical form to contexts of use, unlike the geometrical criteria of drawings, which is a symbolic representation responsive only to itself.

Design methods were intended to overcome the limitations of design-by-drawing and regain some of the adaptability present in craftwork. The central purpose of design methods, as Jones conceived of it, was to permit collaboration in the design process, rather than being limited to the intuitive decisions of individual designers:

The kinds of design skill which are called for in using the newer design methods, which the professions as yet do not seem to take seriously, are suited to collaboration, to the sharing of responsibilities between users and experts, and to designing imaginatively in a collective process, as was the case in craft evolution.[24]

Jones is consistent on this point throughout his work. In *Design Methods* he writes:

The ultimate answer to the dilemma is not for designers to become as gods but for the design process to become more public so that everyone who is affected by design decisions can foresee what can be done and can influence the choices that are made. The purpose of this book is to explore some first attempts at permitting many brains, rather than one, to grasp, and to explore, the complexities of designing.[25]

When interviewed about this point Jones said:

I've always been keen on collaborative design. I think that's the purpose of design methods, to enable people to be creative in groups. That's the purpose. Most of the criticisms and the reaction of the seventies against design methods said it was not necessary or didn't fit individual thinking, particularly of architects, and I say, well it wasn't meant to.[26]

Jones's view of the importance of explicit consideration of users in the design process permeates his work. He remarks, for example:

It is astonishing how much designing goes on in gross ignorance of user requirements.
. . . There is little chance of locating the limits of human performance without careful measurements and there is every chance of completely overlooking, or misunderstanding, user behaviour if no consultation or observation of users precedes designing. . . .
In the writer's opinion nobody should be allowed to practice design until he has subjected himself to the humbling but rewarding experience of seeing how far from reality is his conception of what users really think.[27]

Collaboration was made possible — the design process was to be made public — by making the process explicit and externalizing design thinking. In other words, Jones attempted to redesign the design process itself in such a way that all those people who would be affected by designing could become involved in decision making. Of this he writes:

The first question to be answered is "What do the new methods have in common?" The most obvious answer has already been given: it is that all the methods are attempts to make public the hitherto private thinking of designers; to *externalize* the design process. A major advantage of bringing design thinking into the open is that other people, such as users, can see what is going on and contribute to it information and insights that are outside the designer's knowledge and experience.[28]

Elsewhere he writes, "The benefit of expressing design thinking systematically in terms of 'maps', or 'navigational aids', is to make the early stages of the design process accessible to many people instead of restricting it to an experienced few."[29]

Another major reason for externalizing design thinking was so that both rationality and intuition could be incorporated into the design process. This is clearly set out in a course book written by Chris Crickmay in collaboration with Jones:

Success depends upon being able to mix rational and intuitive thinking. Rational thinking on its own wastes the vast information patterning capacity of the nervous system. Intuition on its own depends too much upon the experience and bias of one designer. A skill must be exercised in choosing between one and the other which could be called meta-intuition, or meta-rationality.[30]

In order to externalize design thinking, to make design a public process, Jones "disintegrates" the design process into three stages: divergence, transformation, and convergence. The traditional breakdown of the design process — analysis, synthesis, and evaluation — was considered by Jones too limited, not providing the opportunity to question the aims of the design process itself. He told me: "I think all of those three fit into the convergence stage myself. I think it's a much longer and wider process. *So it's not another way of doing design, you see, it's another way of doing what designers don't do at all.*"[31] In this sense Jones is expanding the design process, adding to convergence, which constitutes the whole of a traditional design process, two predesign stages: divergence and transformation.

The divergence stage enables everyone involved in the design process to do some unlearning, some *de-signing* as Edwin Schlossberg calls it. The key stage of the design process as conceived of by Jones, however, is transformation, which is "the critical part of all creative acts. The essence of transformation is generating a *new* option or insight that didn't previously exist. Whereas the usual political way of overcoming conflict is compromise, the creative way is transformation, or conflict resolution."[32] This is a critical point; unlike in politics, design done well does not result in compromise. Rather, using the divergence and transformation stages of the design process, an approach that is mutually satisfactory to all of the people to be affected by designing is sought.

The disintegrated design process is, according to Jones, in contrast to the process used by professional designers: "in professional designing, design strategies are to a large extent fixed. The professional designer is committed from the start to a professional strategy leading to a standard solution however much evidence he may encounter on the way to suggest he switches."[33] One of the principal motivations of Jones in his work with design methods was to increase the scope, or the "perceptual span" of designing.

As noted earlier, Jones developed his initial views on design methods while in industry as a means of getting the results of his ergonomics studies incorporated into the design process. After working in industry, however, Jones entered academic life, organizing and conducting a course in Design Technology that focused on developing new approaches to design research and design methods. Jones wrote that this program was

an attempt to extend the education of architects, engineers, and others to include the new applied sciences that are increasingly relevant to designing and planning the physical environment but are not yet included in the conventional training of professional designers and planners. These new sciences, of which the best known are computing, ergonomics (human factors engineering), operations research, systems engineering, and systematic design methods, have been blended together under the title "design technology," to form courses for the Master of Science degree for the University Diploma in Technical Science at the University of Manchester Institute of Science and Technology.

The purpose of this experiment in design education is to find ways of removing the barriers between arts and sciences and between the many professions that are increasingly relevant to design problems. The working principle is to give each student enough experience of the seemingly conflicting methods of science and of design to enable him to resolve the differences within himself. It is argued that the barriers between disciplines and professions are much more easily crossed by persons who understand both sides than by attempts to communicate between persons each of whom knows only one side. The practical aim is to train people for work in inter-disciplinary and interprofessional planning and development teams.[34]

Unfortunately, at the time of Jones' course, the 1960s, industry in Britain was not clamoring for Jones's graduates with interdisciplinary training. As evidenced by recent trends in postindustrial design, however, these skills are now very much needed.

After a decade running the course in design technology, Jones went on to become the first professor of design at the British Open University, an institution whose students do not regularly attend classes but rather work at home, receiving their lectures via television and radio. Jones's stay at the Open University was brief, however. He soon retired from institutional life altogether and began a series of personal design experiments that have occupied him since; these will be discussed subsequently.

Many of the ideas underpinning the design methods movement are extremely important: the role of collaboration, the enhancing of design thinking through the incorporation of rationality and intuition, and the attempt to find alternatives to drawing as the principal mode of design activity. Most significantly, Jones and Alexander recognized the failings and inapplicability of the then contemporary design methods and proposed structural changes to the design process itself to realize designs that better match their contexts of use. That was the idea, anyway. In practice the design-methods movement was a failure and is now, in its original form, a largely abandoned and discredited approach.

Several specific areas can be identified that led to the failure of the design-methods movement. One of the primary complaints was the apparent complexity of much of the early work in the subject. Alexander's set theory and tree diagrams along with Jones's dense text and complex diagrams all looked too analytical, too abstract, too inapplicable to the task of design as then understood. Designers are well known for their aversion to science, so much of the writing on design methods must have seemed foreign. As Jones himself notes:

Perhaps the most characteristic feature of the literature on design methods is the prevalence of block diagrams, matrices and networks of many kinds that resemble, to varying degrees, the diagrams and calculations that computer programmers use. We can regard this mapping of interrelationships as an attempt to find something more tangible than thinking, but less detailed than a scale drawing, with which to portray the complexity of designing at the systems level: a means of giving the systems designer a wide enough "perceptual span."[35]

Maybe, but for a designer or student with a deadline tomorrow this seems to offer little help. Another obstacle to the adoption of design methods was the scholarly orientation of the movement in view of designers' equally famous

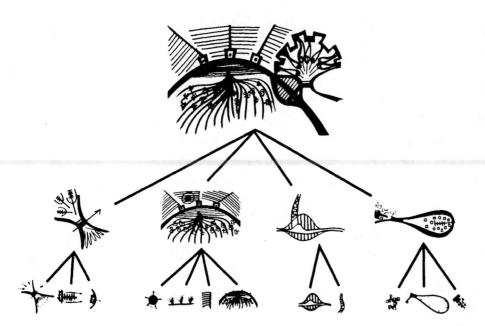

**Christopher Alexander.
Tree Diagram.**
This diagram, from
*Notes on the Synthesis
of Form*, reflects the
design methodologists'
attempt to map ideas in
a way that was more
tangible than thinking
but less detailed than a
scale drawing.

aversion to reading, a condition perhaps understandable in view of the vacuous nature of much of the writing on architecture and design.

The failure of design methods to significantly affect design as practiced cannot be blamed, however, on the designers who didn't take up the subject. There were a few structural problems and mistaken assumptions within the movement itself that are largely responsible for the failure of design methods to affect positively the responsiveness of design to users. There was, for example, a conflict between the founders of the movement — such as Jones and Alexander — who wished to augment designers' intuition with a wider rationality, and those who wished to *replace* intuition with rationality. The latter group, who came to be most numerous in the movement, believed the design task itself to be completely calculable; this is as dangerous and misguided an assumption as we have yet come across in this study. Of this approach Jones writes: "There was a phase in the sixties when many architects had a mania for design methods, but it wasn't everyone that had the mania. I think it was only the rational part of design methods which became popular, and it only became popular with the kind of person who is very keen on rationality."[36] Design methods seem to have been embraced only by those who mistakenly believed design to be a completely explicable, rational proposition. In view of this it is perhaps just as well that the design-methods movement proved to be a practical failure.

Another mistake, common to most approaches to design methods, was the separation of the design task itself into two general stages — analysis and synthesis, or programming and design. The assumption on which this was based, a feature of most design research, is that a design problem can be investigated, understood, in short "known" *before* designing itself takes place. This idea was present, for example, in Alexander's early work:

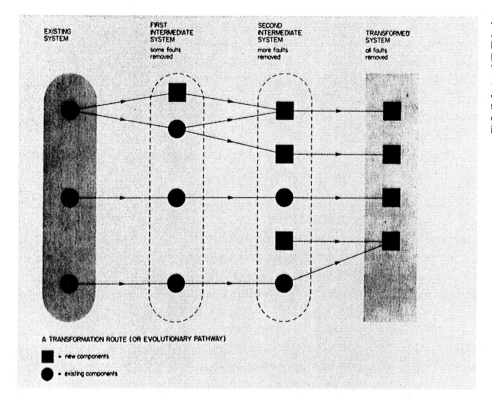

EXISTING SYSTEM / FIRST INTERMEDIATE SYSTEM some faults removed / SECOND INTERMEDIATE SYSTEM more faults removed / TRANSFORMED SYSTEM all faults removed

A TRANSFORMATION ROUTE (OR EVOLUTIONARY PATHWAY)

■ = new components
● = existing components

**John Chris Jones.
A Transformational
Route (or Evolutionary
Pathway).**
This diagram, from
Design Methods, reflects
Jones' desire to repre-
sent the interrelationship
of systems-level design
ideas graphically.

Finding the right design program for a given problem is the first phase of the design process. It is, if we like, the analytical phase of the process. The first phase of the process must of course be followed by the synthetic phase, in which a form is derived from the program. We shall call this synthetic phase *the realization of the program.*[37]

Jones similarly wrote of the pedagogical method for his course in design technology:

The formal teaching is more concerned with principles and methods than with particular design problems. Projects are likewise more concerned with gathering information on which to base design decisions than with making design decisions, i.e. the program is concerned with design research rather than actual designing. The main emphasis, in both teaching and practice, is on the ability to deal formally and precisely with the many uncertainties that present themselves at the start of a design problem.[38]

Jones has since revised his view on this, advocating an interdependency of problem and solution. He now believes that the design task cannot be fully understood in the abstract but rather the "problem" or task can only be proper-ly formed in view of potential solutions or problem synthesis. He writes:

To think of designing as "problem-solving" is to use a rather dead metaphor for a lively process and to forget that design is not so much a matter of adjusting to the status quo as of realising new possibilities and discovering our reactions to them. To make or invent something new is to change not only one's surroundings but to change oneself and the way one perceives: it is to change reality a little. For this reason it is, I believe, a mistake to begin designing by thinking only of the problem, as we'll call it, and to leave the thinking of how it is to be solved to later stages. One's mind, though not one's paper-work, is best kept in a constant intermingling of both problem and solution so that the interdependency of each is evident throughout. The initial expression of objectives, or needs, however abstract and absolute it may seem, is, I think, full of hidden assumptions about how the person stating it thinks it can be satisfied, eg the statement "solve the unemployment problem" could imply that we are to become engaged in a search for jobs of some kind, but an imaginative response may well suggest ways of workless living in which unemployment is no longer the problem. If realised, the inspired solution changes our minds.[39]

The principal failure of design methods, however, was a social one. Like the environment-behavior researchers, design methodologists tended to view their work as a "good thing" that would naturally be taken up once publicized. They gave insufficient attention to the profound social implications of design methods. Specifically, adoption of design methods as they were originally conceived would entail: users being "reeducated" (yet again), organizational changes in design offices, and design methodologists changing their own ideas and roles. In each case the people with the power to change were, at the time, disinclined to do so. Some of the oversights of the design methodologists are shared with other movements. Addressing the need for "reeducation," for example, Jones writes, "The real difficulty is that of re-educating both professional opinion and public opinion to understand and to believe in the new principle of planning, not for what is feasible at the present, but *for what is likely to be feasible* when the plans are put into effect."[40] He does, however, allude to the difficulty of this, while not questioning its desirability: "Once we recognize that ideas are not easily-changed figments of the mind but the necessary prelude to any kind of human action we can see how unlikely it is that one person's new idea will be acted upon by others."[41]

Jones further reveals that design methods could not really be effective without structural change in design offices:

I have previously suggested that a new kind of design organization may be necessary to permit a complete change to systematic work. The elaboration of the preliminary stages of design is likely to require the setting up of specialist predesign sections, which are insulated from day-to-day contingencies and which operate on longer budgeting periods than are normal in design and development. The cost and time of this extra work early in designing would be justified only if the total development costs are lessened, and if the tendency to over-run delivery dates is thereby kept under better control.[42]

The organizational change that Jones prescribed is a reality now, as seen in the "Human Age" design teams in Japan, but was not adopted by British industry in the 1960s. Another difficulty with design methods from a pragmatic point of view is noted by Jones:

The great difficulty of introducing Systematic Design is that its advantages are not obtained in first attempts. Successful application is much more likely when changes in organization have been introduced beforehand. As with many new things it involves an acclimatization period during which things may get worse before they get better.[43]

50

In most cases attempts to use design methods were abandoned *during* the acclimatization process, before any benefits accrued.

Reflecting on the failure, or failures, of the design methods movement to positively affect designing Jones writes:

We sought to be open minded, to make design processes that would be more sensitive to life than were the professional practices of the time. But the result was rigidity: a fixing of aims and methods to produce designs that everyone now feels to be insensitive to human needs. Another result was that design methods became more theoretical and many of those drawn to the subject turned it into the academic study of methods (methodology) instead of trying to design things better. The language used to describe designing, and to describe the aims and purposes of things designed, became more and more abstract. The words lost touch with how it feels to be a designer and how it feels to inhabit the systems being designed. . . .

So the fault in method-making was that we made methods as "products" and handed them on to the designers expecting them to use them, as "tools", as means to an end. Which became a logical trap, turning the idea of process into its opposite? And many designers rejected these tools, which was fortunate, perhaps.[44]

Elsewhere he writes:

In the case of design methods my intention was to find ways to make the design process more sensitive to life but what happened was the imposition of methods that were of a larger scale than those we had before but which are less sensitive. Rationality, originally seen as the means to open up the intuition to aspects of life outside the designer's experience, became, almost overnight, a toolkit of rigid methods that obliged designers and planners to act like machines, deaf to every human cry and incapable of laughter.

. . . our world of design, seems to have driven design methods out of its right place as a practical way of enlivening design and into the sterile function of being a vehicle for some pretty useless and fruitless academic nonsense.[45]

As Jones notes here perhaps the major failing of the design methodologists was their inability, at that time, to do themselves what they were asking everyone else to do — to change *their* aims, to abandon the design of artifacts altogether. As Jones himself admits, "My thought about this, is that, though we saw the need to change the processes of designing we did not see the need to change its aims. We retained the concept of 'product' as the outcome of designing."[46]

At this stage the reader may fairly wonder why so much space has been given to an outdated, failed design approach. Well, for all its many failings there is implicit in the philosophy of design methods, if not in the application of them, the seeds of the most advanced approach to user-sensitive design yet developed. The failure of the design methods movement was not that it went too far, but that it did not go far enough. At the time of its inception even the founders of the movement could not come to terms with the implications of their work. A measure of the underlying vitality of design methods can, however, be gauged by looking at the more recent work of Alexander and Jones, in which they attempt to realize their original intentions in founding the design-methods movement in terms of the knowledge gained from that movement's failure.

THE PATTERN LANGUAGE

Both Christopher Alexander and John Chris Jones reacted against the overrationalization that resulted from their early work with design methods. While they both intended to expand the scope of designing — to improve design — the net result of the design-methods movement was, by their own admission, an increase in the rigidity of the design process and a worsening of the quality of design. Alexander wrote of design methods as originally conceived, "they actually prevent you from being in the right state of mind to do the design."[47] Whereas originally Alexander focused on the rational, explicable side of designing, in his work since that time he has addressed the more qualitative aspects of building. Discussing this approach he said:

I really cannot conceive of a properly formed attitude toward buildings, as an artist or builder, or in any way, if it doesn't ultimately confront the fact that buildings work in the realm of feeling. . . . Actually, it's been my impression that a large part of the history of modern architecture has been a kind of panicked withdrawal from these kinds of feelings, which have governed the formation of buildings over the last 2000 years or so.[48]

In his work over the past two decades Alexander has tried to develop a fairly simple, directly applicable design method through which building tasks could be carried out, a method that possessed this "feeling" that was present in architecture and building until the industrial era. The result of Alexander's work, which was carried out with his team at the Center for Environmental Structure at the University of California, Berkeley, has been the formulation of an explicit "pattern language." In 1977 Alexander and his collaborators published *A Pattern Language*,[49] which consists of 253 patterns ranging from the largest scale — towns — through buildings and down to construction details. Each pattern is given a name, a diagram of its spatial layout, the rationale for its inclusion, and a specification of the links between the given pattern and those related to it at a larger and smaller scale. The strength of Alexander's work is that in the patterns he explicitly links the patterns of events that take place in a space to the layout of the space itself, rather than focusing, as did the designers of the industrial era, on geometrical criteria alone. As he writes:

We must begin by understanding that every place is given its character by certain patterns of events that keep on happening there. These patterns of events are always interlocked with certain geometric patterns in the space. Indeed, as we shall see, each building and each town is ultimately made out of these patterns in the space, and out of nothing else: they are the atoms and the molecules from which a building or a town is made.[50]

Alexander emphasizes this throughout his writings, noting:

Those of us who are concerned with buildings tend to forget too easily that all the life and soul of a place, all of our experiences there, depend not simply on the physical environment, but on the patterns of events which we experience there. . . . We know, then, that what matters in a building or a town is not its outward shape, its physical geometry alone, but the events that happen there. . . . The action and the space are indivisible. The action is supported by this kind of space. The space supports this kind of action. The two form a unit, a pattern of events in space . . . [but] this does not mean that space creates events, or that it causes them.[51]

Citing an example of the interaction between patterns of events and patterns of space, Alexander writes:

Each sidewalk is a unitary system, which includes *both* the field of geometrical relationships which define its concrete geometry, *and* the field of human actions and events, which are associated with it. For since space is made up of these living elements, these labeled patterns of events in space, we see that what seems at first sight like the dead geometry we call a building or town is indeed a quick thing, a living system, a collection of interacting, and adjacent, patterns of events in space, each one repeating certain events over and over again, yet always anchored by its place in space. And, if we hope to understand the life which happens in a building or a town, we must therefore try to understand the structure of space itself.[52]

Alexander emphasizes that his team's book constitutes *a* pattern language, not the only one possible. He views each pattern in the book as a hypothesis, though he feels more confident that some patterns represent underlying, invariant relationships between form and activities than do others. In different cultures and in application to new building tasks new patterns may have to be developed. Moreover, Alexander believes that each of us carry our own pattern language within us that, while largely shared with our culture, is personal and independent. It was these implicit pattern languages that were the source for building and craftwork before geometrical design criteria began to predominate with the onset of industrialization. According to Alexander it is now necessary to rediscover and make explicit pattern languages as a means of reacquainting people — designers and non-designers alike — with what he terms "the timeless way of building":

The people can shape buildings for themselves, and have done it for centuries, by using languages which I call pattern languages. A pattern language gives each person who uses it, the power to create an infinite variety of new and unique buildings, just as his ordinary language gives him the power to create an infinite variety of sentences.

But in our time the languages have broken down. Since they are no longer shared, the processes which keep them deep have broken down: and it is therefore virtually impossible for anybody, in our time, to make a building live. . . .

In a traditional culture, these patterns exist as independent entities within your mind, but it is not necessary for you to recognize them as separate atomic units, nor to know them by name, nor to be able to speak about them. It is no more necessary than it is for you to be able to describe the rules of grammar in the language which you speak. However, in a period when languages are no longer widely shared, when people have been robbed of their intuitions by specialists, when they no longer even know the simplest patterns that were once implicit in their habits, it becomes necessary to make patterns explicit, precisely and scientifically, so that they can be shared in a new way — explicitly, instead of implicitly — and discussed in public.[53]

In contrast to the traditional use of implicit patterns, Alexander writes:

In the early phases of industrial society which we have experienced recently, the pattern languages die. Instead of being widely shared, the pattern languages which determine how a town gets made become specialized and private. Roads are built by highway engineers; buildings by architects; parks by planners; hospitals by hospital consultants; schools by educational specialists; gardens by gardeners; tract housing by developers. The people of the town themselves know hardly any of the languages which these specialists use. And if they want to find out what these languages contain, they can't, because it is considered professional expertise. The professionals guard their language jealously to make themselves indispensable. Even within any one profession, professional jealousy keeps people from sharing their pattern languages. Architects, like chefs, jealously guard their recipes, so that they can maintain a unique style to sell. The languages start out by being specialized, and hidden from the people; and then within the specialties, the languages become more private still, and hidden from one another, fragmented. . . .

Those few patterns which do remain within our languages become degenerate and stupid. This follows naturally from the fact that the languages are so highly specialized. The users, whose direct experience once formed the languages, no longer have enough contact to influence them. This is almost bound to happen, as soon as the task of building passes out of the hands of the people who are most directly concerned, and into the hands of people who are not doing it for themselves, but instead for others. So long as I build for myself, the patterns I use will be simple, and human, and full of feeling, because I understand my situation. But as soon as the few people begin to build for "the many," their patterns about what is needed become abstract; no matter how well meaning they are, their ideas gradually get out of touch with reality, because they are not faced daily with the living examples of what the patterns say.[54]

This, Alexander explains, is because "experts try to make towns and buildings which are adapted to people's needs, but they are always trivial. They can only deal with general forces, which are common to all men, and never with the particular forces that make one particular man unique and human."[55]

Central to the use of pattern languages is the concept of repair. For Alexander this is not an attempt to regain an ideal state, but rather to discover one. In this sense a building when built is at best a hypothesis, one that must be tested and modified by those who will use it. This is the "repair" to which Alexander refers. The pattern languages provide the medium through which building users can participate directly in the formation of environments to suit their activities:

No building is ever perfect. Each building, when it is first built, is an attempt to make a self-maintaining whole configuration. But our predictions are invariably wrong. People use buildings differently from the way they thought they would. And the larger the pieces become, the more serious this is. The process of design, in the mind's eye, or on the site, is an attempt to simulate in advance, the feeling and events which will emerge in the real building, and to create a configuration which is in repose with respect to these events. But the prediction is all guesswork; the real events which happen there are always at least slightly different; and the larger the building is, the more likely the guesses are to be inaccurate. It is therefore necessary to keep changing the buildings, according to the real events which actually happen there. And the larger the complex of buildings, neighborhood, or town, the more essential it is for it to be built up gradually, from thousands of acts, self-correcting acts, each one improving and repairing the acts of the others. . . .

This goes vastly beyond the normal conception of repair. In the commonplace use of the word repair, we assume that when we repair something, we are essentially trying to get it back to its original state. This kind of repair is patching, conservative, static. But in this new use of the word repair, we assume, instead, that every entity is changing constantly: and that at every moment we use the defects of the present state as the starting point for the definition of the new state.[56]

Alexander writes further:

The prismatic buildings of our own time, the buildings built with the simple geometry of cubes, and circles, spheres, and spirals, and rectangles; this geometry is the naive order, created by the childish search for order. We happen to think of this order as the proper order for a building, because we have been taught to think so; but we are wrong. The proper order for a building or a town, which comes about when buildings are correctly fitted to the forces in them, is a much richer order, with a far more complex geometry. But it is not merely rich and complex; it is also very specific. And it will show itself, under any circumstances, where buildings are actually correct. Whenever anyone manages to make a building which is alive, it will have this specific character, because that is the only character which is compatible with life.[57]

The design-methods movement, as originally conceived, often led to a situation John Chris Jones terms "method over mind," in which slavish adherence to design-methods procedures removed all humanity — all thoughts and feelings — from the design process. In view of this Alexander is very careful to point out that the pattern language is not an end in itself, but rather is a means to an end:

This ageless character has nothing, in the end, to do with languages. The language, and the processes which stem from it, merely release the fundamental order which is native to us. They do not teach us, they only remind us of what we know already, and of what we shall discover time and time again, when we give up our ideas and opinions, and do exactly what emerges from ourselves. . . .

So paradoxically you learn that you can only make a building live when you are free enough to reject even the very patterns which are helping you. The more I watch our pattern language being used, the more I realize that the language does not teach people new facts about their environment. It awakens old feelings. It gives people permission to do what they have always known they wanted to do, but have shunned, in recent years, because they have been frightened and ashamed by architects who tell them that it is not "modern." People are afraid of being laughed at, for their ignorance about "art"; and it is this fear which makes them abandon their own stable knowledge of what is simple and right.[58]

I have quoted at length from Alexander because he so clearly sets out his views on the nature and importance of pattern languages. In his analysis he demonstrates how the patterns now used by designers are oversimplified, solely based on geometry, and isolated from the needs and experience of users. In contrast, Alexander, in his pattern language, explicitly links the patterns of events that take place in a space — its use — with the patterns of space that house the activity, rather than focusing on geometry alone. The philosophy behind the pattern language constitutes a fundamental challenge to all of the mainstream design approaches that have emerged since modernism. Through use of the pattern language the design process is radically transformed; the principal benefit is that the people affected by designing become empowered to shape their environments for themselves.

DESIGN AS A RESPONSE TO THE WHOLE OF LIFE

Like Alexander, John Chris Jones reacted strongly against what became of design methods. To his regret, rather than improving design in practice, as he had originally intended, design methods became an overly rationalized, academic pursuit. In fact where the methods were used they often made things worse, eliminating intuition and imagination from the design process rather than encouraging them. Responding to what had become of design methods in practice, Jones wrote:

I have to admit that, where they have been used, new methods such as system-designing, computing, etc, have made life more rigid, more homogenized, less human. . . .

My thoughts about the subject have not changed since, in the late forties, I found myself drawn to find ways in which it might be possible to make the man-made world of machines and industrial living better fitted to human life. . . . But something has gone wrong. In ways that are clearer to me now than when I wrote [*Design Methods*] this wealth of new thinking seems not to have had the effects expected, at least by myself. Instead of being the means by which professional practices in design and other fields could be despecialized and made more sensitive to human needs the new methods have become convenient tools for larger and more rigid planning and have also become the means of making design into a barren academic subject removed from life, from the lives of those for whose benefit it's supposed to exist, ourselves as consumers and users of industrial products. More and more we recognise ourselves not as users of industrial life but as non-persons, tools, objects that are used by the system. What has gone wrong?[59]

Jones states further:

So to me now, as in the past, the purpose of seeking changes in methods not only in design but in all departments of life is to change the pattern of life as we make it, artificially and collectively, not to support the status quo and the inhumanization we inherit but to permit the composing of a form of life that is free of the errors of specialization and of alienation. To make a way of living that is beautiful, (can laws be beautiful, can work, can millions of people act together as trusted friends not as distrusting manipulators of each other's lives?), to attempt the best we can imagine and to use all intelligence to make it real.[60]

Jones's beliefs, which led him to undertake design methods in the first place, have not fundamentally changed, but the nature and the scope of his work is now radically different. He writes:

Since 1968 I have found myself leaving most of what, up till then, I had been doing. I left design methods, feeling that it had become a rigid and inhuman activity, and I left academic life, at the Open University, feeling that that too had become rigid and inhuman. And now there are many critics of design methods, as applied to architecture, who imply that the rigidity came from the misconceptions of those, like myself, who foisted mechanical ways of thinking onto the architectural profession, which thus lost some of its freedom. The methods did not fit the mind. . . .

What I suddenly recaptured was the conviction that, whatever may have become of design methods in recent years, the original intentions of those of us who tried to improve design processes, ten or more years ago, was to respond to the connectedness of everything. To cease splitting life into fragments, particularly when it is people and the experience of life that is being fragmented. I realised that the intention of the new methods, (mine anyway, and I think its true of many others) was to overcome the limitations of professional procedures in all the design professions. Their inability to respond to life itself, which was becoming the object of design, as the extent of what is man-made grew and grew. . . .

Collective inventiveness, and intelligence: that seems to be the quality most needed in design, a quality without which the new design methods are ineffective. The ability to act on intuition, with suspended judgement. To risk, to enjoy, to learn from, the finding out of the extent to which one's picture of reality can change . . . that's not something one can do on a drawing board, or by computer simulations of behaviour. You have to live it. . . .

When I took leave of design I was reacting against what I called the "inhuman" use of abstract functional language to describe and fix life in the dreary and numbing formulae of design methodologists, environmentalists, ecologists, and others. Somehow, I felt, my friends, those with the good intentions of improving life, have become the enemies of mankind, of ourselves as persons.[61]

When I questioned Jones on his present view of design methods he said, "Forget the methods until you get the atmosphere right, then choose a method that fits *that*."[62]

Jones concluded that the failure of the design methods to affect designing positively, as had been intended, could be traced to the fact that the design methodologists themselves had not fully recognized that for design methods to be adopted the goals and nature of the design process itself would have to be changed — that the problems with design were not technical or procedural but rather personal and social. In reacting against design methods Jones left his job at the Open University and began independently to pursue experiments exploring a wider view of design, "at the scale of modern life,"[63] a view of "designing WITHOUT A PRODUCT . . . as a process or way of living in itself."[64]

Since the early seventies Jones has been pursuing this radically expanded vision of the design process through experiments with the "time arts" — films, performance plays, poetry, fictions — and through exploration of new publication formats, such as photocopies, microfiche, and computer disks and networks, as means of using new technology in a personal way. He wanted to ensure that his work was no longer simply *about* design, but instead *was* design itself, a reflection of the ideas within it. It is important to recognize that Jones's new direction was not in fact a repudiation of design methods themselves, nor of the motivations behind them; rather it reflected a belated recognition of the social aspects of design that, ironically, had been the purpose of the movement initially.

Like Alexander, Jones in his current work is focusing more on the feeling, the atmosphere, brought about through the use of methods, rather than overtly addressing the methods themselves. Whereas Alexander, in developing the pattern language, focused on relating patterns of events to patterns of space for different scales of building tasks, Jones has abandoned the design of physical artifacts altogether, instead conducting personal experiments that explore new ways of living. Of this transition Jones writes:

If, as I think now, the main purpose of "the design process" is collective learning, the deliberate seeking of new ways of living, then we must expect to make changes in our processes and procedures (for this learning often takes the form of sudden insights). . . .

It is time that we begin to de-mechanize our lives, that we dismantle the monstrous extension of production methods to life itself, as if we, and everything else, existed only as a means and never as an end, never as something good in itself. In design, this undoing of the mistakes of our industrial past can begin, not by abandoning goals altogether, but by switching from fixed goals to variable ones.[65]

In his recent work Jones begins by changing his own mind, his own ways of working, his own way of living, rather than simply prescribing approaches for others to follow.

Earlier in his career Jones sought to overcome the limitations of engineering by taking up the then emerging field of industrial design. Upon recognizing the superficial, style-oriented nature of industrial design, however, he took up ergonomics as a means of more effectively accounting for user requirements in design. When his ergonomics data weren't incorporated into engineering designs, he developed design methods as a means of integrating rationality and intuition explicitly in the design process. From industry he went into education, first in a traditional setting, then in a potentially innovative one. Upon recognizing, with disappointment, what had become of the design methods movement, Jones retired to initiate his series of personal experiments in an attempt to make design responsive to life as a whole, as a means of transcending the fragmentation of experience common to industrial life:

Generally design seems to be becoming a social art and to do this properly it seems we need to learn from experimental artists whose happenings and other events are making art a way of living. Both art and design at last seem like meeting, across the Cartesian split of mind from body, to enable us to find a new genius for collaboration not in the making of products and systems and bureaucracies but in the composing of contexts that include everyone, designers too. To be a part. To find how to make all we do and think relate to all we sense and know, (not merely to attend to fragments of ourselves and our situations.)[66]

In the early 1970s Jones began to study the work of experimental artists such as John Cage, whose work with chance processes constituted an attempt to erase the distinction between composer and audience. The element of chance in Cage's compositions makes everyone present both a listener and, in a sense, a creator of each piece. Similarly, Jones adopted the use of chance processes to open up his writing to influences outside his own intuition, as a means of bringing more of the world into his work. Jones uses, for example, the *I-Ching or Book of Changes*, an oracle that is essentially an interactive book of philosophy and that is consulted via chance process. Of this he writes:

Although, in using the *I Ching*, I've often had what seem, at first, to be magical coincidences, I've realised with much experience of the book and of using chance in composition, and in living, that what it does is to enable one to be aware of a mass of connections, between all we experience, that is hidden by our intentions. It's not that the oracle is uniquely the cause or trigger of what one then sees is happening: it is I'd say the means of losing the engrossment in one's purposes and thoughts that hides what is happening, makes one unable to look.[67]

Another chance technique Jones adopted from Cage is the use of random numbers as a compositional tool. While Cage advocates pure chance, or indeterminacy, Jones's application is more modest; he calls it "systematic chance" and uses it to select quotes, for example, from five different sources with which he has empathy for inclusion in a text. Sometimes he also uses chance to determine the placement of the quotes in the text, which results in "prepared pages" that frame and precede the writing he does himself. Jones always includes the relevant context for any quote selected by chance and will, on rare occasions, reject the results of the chance process. Though it might sound from this description as though the use of chance is simply the result of laziness or carelessness or mental bankruptcy of some sort, it can actually be a very enlivening process that is, according to Jones, "applicable to anything that has to be organized before one can experience it."[68]

Jones describes the process of using chance in composition:

I find, as always, during the tiny drama of seeing what comes next (which makes chance processes more interesting to operate than to see the results of) that I lose all ability to react to the words as a reader of the text I am composing. Even now, minutes later, it has a not-from-me quality that is nice, and a quality of nobody, me included, having been in on its composition, and so not yet having understood it, or "read" it in the sense of letting it form what meanings it can in my mind. The writer becomes a reader, no more informed than any other. That, I think, is very nice. Also the fact that anyone can do it, provided they have some sensitivity to the making of the initial decision of what to sample, what text or repertoire of items, and of what constitutes a unit of sampling.[69]

One of my students, Lew Neuman, composed a performance play using the method of chance processes developed by Jones. In this play, *A Revolution of the Senses: A Play on the Future of Design*, Neuman used chance to select from the writings of Jones, Andrea Branzi, and John Cage, as well as the artists Brian Eno and Christo, both of whose work will be discussed later. I was taken aback by the appropriateness of the "randomly" selected quotes that resulted from the chance process, as well as the aptness of their sequence and relationship to one another. I will mention too, because it is not always the case, that not only was the use of chance invigorating and enjoyable to Lew and me, but the audience for his play enjoyed it as well. When they were afterward told the process used many found it truly difficult to believe that it had not been composed in a traditional, meaning-oriented way.

Addressing the benefits of the use of chance Jones writes:

I suppose using chance processes is no different in principle than for instance deciding to use the sonnet form. What it does is to enable one to operate one's intuitions at a larger scale than usual, to compose using a far larger range of sources than is in one's memory, in detail, and is outside the capacity of one's word-producing-and-choosing process-skill to do itself. BUT, I find repeatedly, that after some hours/days/months of persistent and seemingly dumb-headed attempts at composing thus, one's intuitive process of word-and-thought-making-and choosing is much improved, more catholic, and one has learnt not to censor one's words etc and to accept as relevant much that one could not use before.[70]

Jones's recent direction has been heavily criticized by those who feel he has abandoned the cause of design methods, retreated into an individual backwater of insignificance, or simply gone off the deep end. And while it's true that Jones has made few concessions to ready intelligibility, either personally or through his work, it is equally true that his recent work has profound implications for the organization of postindustrial life, if one chooses to accept them.

Jones's focus now is on experimental living in which "design" is conceived of in the broadest sense — as a response to life as a whole. In a sense Jones's experiments with approaches to postindustrial living are analogous to William Morris's earlier attempts to find ways of coping with life in the industrial era. In comparing his expanded vision of designing to previous design research approaches, Jones writes:

Design research, in the sense of confronting "what is", does not tell us all we need to learn in deciding how to shape the new. My picture of the improved design research we need now is of experimental villages, cities, networks, etc, in which it *is* possible to explore and experience the social and personal changes that can accompany new products, systems and environments.[71]

3. From Product to Process Design

As has been demonstrated, the principal concern of most designers, whatever trend they associate themselves with, is the adherence to certain geometrical criteria. The designers' view is in sharp contrast to that of users, who are concerned with how well a design works. In short we may contrast the designers' view, which is static and object dependent — product based — with design users' requirements, which are dynamic and experiential — process based. John Chris Jones writes of the design professions: "As professionals . . . we are . . . tied to thinking of the product as central and the users as existing only in relation to what we provide. 'We are here to help the others: what the others are for I've no idea'. This is product-thinking, the not always laughable weakness of industrial life."[1] As long as the success criteria of designers and the public they are to serve differ so greatly there is little chance of design being successful.

Designers' efforts have not resolved the issues raised by industrialization but instead have worsened them. The piecemeal aggregation of designed objects, with little regard to their contexts of use or their aftereffects, has led to some of the most pressing of contemporary problems. The designs for automobiles, for example, are judged by criteria such as styling, performance, efficiency, and status-conferring power. Highway systems, parking lots, garages, and so on are developed independently to cope with the ever-growing number of cars. But the design of the elements of the system as products, as objects, in isolation from one another, has led to a range of problems that have not been adequately addressed. The most serious of these problems is traffic accidents, which claim roughly the same number of lives each year in the United States as were lost by Americans in battle during the whole of the Vietnam War (about 48,000). In addition, there are traffic jams and parking problems brought on by the inability of the system to cope with such an influx of cars. Further, the manufacture and operation of cars leads to pollution and resource depletion. So rather than providing a means of coping with industrialization, the billions of hours of product-design effort spent on the automobile have merely made matters worse.

Other examples of the failure of product-based design to provide an adequate response to industrialization abound, notably environmental pollution as an unforeseen (or disregarded) outcome of the industrial process. Another is the failure, as earlier demonstrated, of architects to provide comfortable, desirable housing — the deconstructivist architects have stopped even trying to do so, constructing buildings to complement modern man's sense of alienation, as they see it. Perhaps, however, this alienation is not an intrinsic quality of the age, but rather results from living in a world that has been fragmented into individual products or things, a world that has been *objectified* with little regard to the connections — the *human* connections — that are, or should be, of preeminent importance in any design effort. As Jones writes:

At what point do we recognise that centralized designing ceases to be effective and becomes an obstacle, and not the means, to "good design". Surely there is such a point. I believe we have already passed beyond it and that it is time to rethink designing, design education, and the need for design professions, in relation to the growing dissatisfaction with technology, design, planning, and their effects. The new competence which the situation now requires is, I believe, not that of deciding the shape of a product of system but the shape of a new context or process in which everyone, not just designers or experts, is enabled to see what is needed of him or her if the form of industrial life is to get better, for everyone, and not worse. To arrive at this is not to continue to design but to do something at a different scale from that, the scale of the whole problem, the scale of decentral action, thought, imagination.[2]

If a single culprit can be blamed for the developments in design since industrialization it must be the two-dimensional scale drawing. The drawing allowed the immediacy of craftwork to slip away and replaced it with a means that was isolated both from the users of design and from the contexts of its use. Drawings permitted larger projects to be undertaken and a division of labor in the planning and making of things. The result of this was that almost all of the important design decisions were taken away from those with immediate knowledge of the product — users and makers — and given to someone who operated according to a static, geometric criteria — the only possible criteria against which to test the "success" of a drawing on the board. In craftwork, on the other hand, the medium of design and its object were the same, they could be tested in the actual context in which they were to be used via trial and error to ensure a "goodness of fit" with both context of use and users.

Goodness of fit was not realized, nor even attempted, in the design of the industrial era. In recent years the flaws in the design process since industrialization have become increasingly apparent. The failures of the industrial design process have been further highlighted by the emergence of new, postindustrial design tasks, such as the design of computer software, to which the design methods of the industrial age, such as drawing, are totally inapplicable. The new postindustrial design tasks are increasingly process-oriented. The focus of the new tasks is on the dynamic experience of users, not on product design per se. As we have seen, companies are increasingly trying to develop products that are more responsive to users, in which user wishes are of foremost importance, realizing William Morris's vision of making technology the servant and not the master of people. In Japan, for example, "humanware" products are now evolved by interdisciplinary product planning teams that concentrate on adapting products to the lifestyle of design users, rather than having a single designer present his or her intuitive "creation" as a fait accompli.

Clearly a new approach to design is needed — one in which the world is viewed not as an aggregate of ill-fitting objects, but rather as a collection of dynamic processes centered on the experience of people. In place of drawings, there must arise a way of looking at how all the objects produced fit together in the widest sense — in their context of use and with their users. Design research was developed to address the perceived failures of the industrial-design process, but most design-research approaches have been ineffective, failing to provide workable alternatives to existing design processes. The design-methods movement, though itself a failure, contained within it the seeds of a new, user-sensitive approach to design. The two founders of the movement, Jones and Alexander, have, in rather different ways, done the most to develop the ideas implicit in the original design-methods movement.

Through the development of the pattern language, Alexander has provided a tool directly applicable to environmental design, which explicitly links the activities that take place in a space — the patterns of events — with the physical forms in which the activities are housed — the patterns of space. Alexander's purpose is to overcome the exclusively geometrical focus of the industrial-design process, to transcend the limitations of design-by-drawing as a design method, and to permit collaboration by everyone, designers and nondesigners alike, in the design process.

Jones, on the other hand, in his recent work has rejected the design of artifacts altogether, choosing to pursue instead "intangible designs" in which the design of experience over time is itself the focus. As noted earlier, Jones believes that the chief failure of the design-methods movement was the failure to change the aims of the design process, the failure to question whether products need always be the outcome of the design process. Through his individual experiments with what he terms "design in space and time," in which he adopts methods from avant-garde artists, Jones demonstrates that designing need not always be linked to the planning of products or objects.

As seen from the failure of the design philosophies since industrialization, and in view of the post-design-methods developments of Alexander and Jones, the product orientation in design is of increasingly limited usefulness. We have reached a major juncture: the nature and purpose of the design process are changing. "Design" itself is being redefined in terms of design users' experience, not geometrical criteria.

Jones began his book *Design Methods* with the question "What is designing?" He reviewed a range of definitions and concluded at that time that design was "the initiation of change in man-made things."[3] But even then he noted, "The objectives of designing become less concerned with the product itself and more concerned with the changes that manufacturers, distributors, users, and society as a whole, are expected to make in order to adapt to, and benefit from, the new design."[4] Similarly in *Notes on the Synthesis of Form* Alexander wrote that "the ultimate object of design is form,"[5] though when Alexander speaks of form he means one that is well fitted to the context in which it is used. Nonetheless, these definitions reflect the limited view with which the founders of the design-methods movement began.

Following his experience with design methods Jones radically altered his own thinking:

A potter modelling a piece of clay into the "perfect" shape for a cup is an ancient, and I think unhelpful, metaphor for the process of designing. When design was limited to the shaping of objects it perhaps sufficed, but now, when the scale has grown to that of systems of objects, and the activities of people, the metaphor has become destructive. We are not clay, not infinitely malleable, not dead. What is the right metaphor now?[6]

Hints of what he believes the right approach might be are given in the course book he wrote in collaboration with Chris Crickmay:

What I shall describe here is a view of *what design might be like if applied in a wider context than it is now*. In so doing I feel that I have brought from design something that could make all activities imaginative, perhaps the quality they have lost most through industrialization. In fact the end result of the process may well be constructive inaction rather than destructive action, because a major intention is to avoid doing the wrong thing in the wrong place at the wrong time.[7]

Recall that the Bronx Development Center was, according to one informed observer, "the wrong concept at the wrong time in the wrong place"[8] and the need for a new, wider, and more user-sensitive conception of design becomes clear.

In the preface to his book *Designing Designing*, which recorded the results of the first decade of Jones's individual design experiments, he notes:

In my earlier book [*Design Methods*] I defined design as the initiation of change in man-made things. Looking now at that definition I still like the emphasis on change but not the assumption that design is limited to the thinking of a few on behalf of many. Nor do I like the assumption that it is to do with change in things but not in ourselves. In my re-thinkings of the nature of design in these pages I have moved far from the picture of "it" as the specialised activity of paid experts who shape the physical and abstract forms of industrial life which we all as consumers accept or adapt to. That notion cannot possibly last for ever — it's too limiting, too insensitive to the reactions it provokes. It's too inert. Designing, if it is to survive as an activity through which we transform our lives, on earth, and beyond, has itself to be redesigned, continually. As do all the other false stabilities, ideas of order, which we inherit or construct, as stepping-stones, no more, useful as they may be at this moment. The turning of creative activity upon itself, attempting to change its nature, our own, is to me the most surprising, the most promising, of the changes to be noticed now, not only in design but as a general tendency.[9]

Citing examples of the new conceptions of design, Jones writes:

Alongside the old idea of design as the drawing of objects that are then to be built or manufactured there are many new ideas of what it is, all very different:

designing as the process of devising not individual products but whole systems or environments such as airports, transportation, hypermarkets, educational curricula, broadcasting schedules, welfare schemes, banking systems, computer networks;

design as participation, the involvement of the public in the decision making process;

design as creativity, which is supposed to be potentially present in everyone;

design as an educational discipline that unites arts and sciences and perhaps can go further than either;

and now the idea of designing WITHOUT A PRODUCT, as a process or way of living in itself . . . (a way out of consumerism?)

I suppose there are other views too but these are enough to let one see how quickly the notion has been changing and how far-reaching are its newer implications.[10]

The term *design* itself becomes problematic when discussing these new views of design. As Jones writes in the revised edition of *Design Methods*:

The word "design" is a big obstacle to understanding what this book is about. "The design of WHAT?" people ask, when they hear of it, and look a little incredulous when I tell them that it is supposed to be about the design of "everything". This reply is misleading because it implies that design methods are intended only for the design of "things", physical objects, and are a substitute for the specialized knowledge and skills of architects, engineers, industrial designers, etc. It is truer to say that design methods are intended for the design of "all-things-together", the "total situation" as I called it in the original introduction, meaning the functions and uses of things, the "systems" into which they are organised, or the "environments" in which they operate. These larger entities, which are hardly "things" in that they can seldom be touched, or seen-as-a-whole, are what I mean by "intangible design". But they are, more so than the objects and products within them, the operating wholes of which modern life is being formed and made: traffic systems, computer software, educational programs, hypermarkets, etc. This is the scale of design today. . . . The change in scale, from physical objects to intangible systems and environments, is also a change from designing-in-space to designing-in-space-and-time."[11]

The principal transition in this new focus for the design process — the broadening of the definition of design — is from a concern with products to a focus on processes. As Jones writes:

The shift from the idea of "progress" (towards a goal, a product) to the ideas of "process" (as all there is) is surely a main event of the twentieth century, in all fields of endeavour. The design methods movement can be seen as our modest version of this historic change ("us" being designers, architects, engineers, etc). The change, in physics, was from the idea of space, time, atom, etc, as finalities, as objects, to seeing them as mobile processes, events. In art, the fixities of "object", "meaning", etc, were abandoned for the notion of "the act of painting" or "the act of looking at it" as being the "art". So far, in design, we have gone only part way (no doubt because in changing how we act, we affect not only perceptions and ideas, but also the technologies upon which everyone relies). We've changed from "planning product" to "planning process" but we've yet to admit that designing could become not goal-seeking but shared imaginative living, end-in-itself.[12]

Whereas product planning or "design in space," with its static, geometrical criteria, was the focus of the traditional design process, planning process or "design in space and time" necessitates consideration of users' dynamic experiences. Jones counsels, "At this point designers need to acknowledge their relative ignorance of 'temporal design' and can perhaps learn from the 'time arts' (music, dance, theater, film, novel, poetry, etc) how to compose-in-time with some sense of beauty,"[13] as he himself has done in his own work.

Jones's views constitute a fundamental challenge to design as we know it, but he is not alone in suggesting that "design" itself must be redefined, and he is not alone in his belief that the proper focus of the design process is users' experience, not physical form. Ralph Caplan, for example, says of the work of Charles and Ray Eames:

To me the most interesting and most sanguine of contemporary design movements is the shift in design attention from objects to situations. The shift is subtle, a matter of emphasis rather than a new departure. For Charles and Ray Eames it is simply the continuation of their approach to problems. For a while the problems they dealt with were solvable by objects. When they shifted their interest to problems that were not solvable by objects, they began making films.[14]

In addition to the recognition of the changing focus of design, Caplan's quote reveals that for this transition to take place the methods and processes of design will themselves have to change.

Similarly, in discussing the work of the Italian radical architecture movements in the 1960s, Andrea Branzi writes:

Mistrust of architecture and the instruments of planning was growing; the now open crisis in the Modern Movement came to be seen as a final day of reckoning, symptom of mortal illness in a discipline that, born as the most advanced point of the system, had become its most backward sector. We even began to ask ourselves whether present-day society was still dealing with the problems of managing its own urban and territorial form through architecture, or whether this historical role had not now been taken over by other instruments and other disciplines.

It had been discovered that doing architecture did not just mean making houses, or constructing useful things in general, but signified expressing oneself, communicating, arguing and freely creating one's own cultural habitat, according to the instinctive right that every individual has to create his own environment, but from which the division of labour in society had totally alienated him. Doing architecture became an activity of free expression, just as making love means not just producing children but communicating through sex.[15]

The belief in the preeminence of process also underlies Christopher Alexander's work with the pattern language:

For once we recognize that much of what we think of as an "element" in fact lies in the pattern of relationships between this thing and the things in the world around it, we then come to the second even greater realization, that the so-called element is itself nothing but a myth, and that indeed, the element itself is not just embedded in a pattern of relationships, but is *itself* entirely a pattern of relationships, and nothing else. The patterns are not just patterns of relationships, but patterns of relationships among other smaller patterns, which themselves have still other patterns hooking them together — and we see finally, that the world is entirely made of all these interhooking, interlocking nonmaterial patterns.[16]

Alexander maintains that the characteristic of the timeless way of building, the quality without a name:

cannot be made, but only generated by a process. It can flow from your actions; it can flow with the greatest ease; but it cannot be made. It cannot be contrived, thought out, designed. It happens when it flows out from the process of creation of its own accord. But we must give up altogether the idea that it is something we can capture, consciously, by working over drawings at the drawing board.[17]

This process can be brought about through the use of a pattern language, which:

guides the acts of all the individuals there in such a way that every act of building, and each smaller act which seems more modest too, is guided by the patterns in the language which are necessary to it, and gradually generates these patterns, day by day, continuously, so that this place is kept alive, continuously, by the gradual process of creation and destruction. It is not the end product of this process which is alive, but the incessant flux itself. There is no product of this process: the buildings and the town, which live, are that incessant flux, which, guided by its language, constantly creates itself.[18]

Jones writes similarly:

So . . . building is a form of living and living is a form of building. That's one way of realising that there are no products, no fixities, only continuous flux. And that designing, making, and using are all processes that are added to, and interact with, the natural processes of the places where these activities occur.[19]

The transition from product to process design is analogous in many respects to the difference in world view reflected in the English and Chinese languages. As Alan Watts writes, "In English the differences between things and actions are clearly, if not always logically, distinguished, but a great number of Chinese words do duty for both nouns and verbs — so that one who thinks in Chinese has little difficulty in seeing that objects are also events, that our world is a collection of processes rather than entities."[20] As with the Chinese understanding of their world, there is an increasing need, in the postindustrial era, to recognize that products do not really exist in isolation from the processes of use that give them their value and meaning. The world of design, like the Chinese world, now needs to be seen as a collection of processes, rather than of products.

In addition to the existing design problems of the industrial age cited earlier, new, postindustrial design tasks, such as computer software, can more usefully be viewed through the experiences of design users, rather than in terms of objects' physical characteristics or the technology involved in them. Jones reinforces this point:

Aims, purposes, requirements, functions: these are words for how we see what's needed. But when we name we tend to exclude the main part, the least predictable: ourselves, our minds, and how they change, once we experience something. It's ourselves, not our words, that are the real purpose of designing. The biggest mistake is to take the product alone as the aim. It's always secondary, always a means, to process, to what we're doing now or will be doing later.[21]

In place of the traditional, object-oriented conception of design, a proliferation of definitions of design has arisen in which the words *design* and *designing* are qualified in terms of the intention behind design. No longer is designing seen as a unitary activity for the planning of objects; rather the new and varied definitions of design reflect the multiplicity of possible outcomes of the design process and, more importantly, the way in which users' experiences are accounted for in the process.

The proliferation of definitions, or qualifications, of design is perhaps analogous to the range of terms for different qualities of consciousness that are central to the philosophy of Yoga. The more intimately one is acquainted with a phenomenon, the more nuances of meaning can be distinguished. So as user experience becomes more central to designing, the quality of that experience can be more fully identified. As in Yoga itself, a central theme for the new definitions of design is *awareness* — the awareness of the processes, implications, and outcomes of designing — design users and contexts included. Within the disparate new approaches to design I have identified three distinct trends, all derived from Jones' work: collaborative design, contextual design, and intangible design.

Collaborative design does not simply constitute the participation of users in a designer's process, nor is it collaboration solely among designers; rather it is a means through which designers and nondesigners alike may participate as equal partners in the design process, shaping not only the outcomes but the aims of designing as well. Jones writes of the relationship of design methods to collaborative design:

I think this is the crux of the matter: the new methods *permit* collaborative designing whereas the old methods do *not*. They change the nature of designing, or can if one lets them. The essential point is that the new methods permit collaboration before "the concept", the organizing idea, the back-of-the-envelope sketch. . . . The new methods, properly used, release everyone from the tyranny of imposed ideas and enable each to contribute to and to act upon, the best that everyone is capable of imagining and doing. This is not easy. It requires not only new methods but a new conception of self.[22]

Contextual design is the design not of objects themselves but rather of contexts — dynamic conditions or situations. The term *contextual design* as used here is distinct from the more limited use of the term by some postmodern architects in their attempt to fit their work into its surroundings. Contextual design is done as a catalyst to user experience, usually aesthetic experiences. Jones writes of contextual design:

It is unlikely that "design participation", the sharing of the process of design with those affected by its results, will make much difference until the nature of designing itself is changed, e.g. by transferring *responsibility* from designers to makers and users. Such a change is happening spontaneously in computing, where software designers are also the makers, and can be users too. It has happened intentionally in music, where some composers have given up control of the sounds to be heard when performers react to scores which do not indicate notes, or tempo, but perhaps only duration, type of instrument, or state of mind. "The composer becomes a listener" as John Cage says. So does the performer. And the audience has to be far more creative than it was before. "But this is not music" say the critics. It is, if you accept that we are capable of changing our minds, of learning to enjoy sounds which formerly we'd have ignored, beauties unexpected. I believe that this big shift in the responsibilities of composers, performers, and audiences is a good model of what is needed now in design: a change *from* the specifying of geometry, physical form, *to* the making of a context, a situation, in which it is possible for others, for us all as users, makers, imaginers, to determine the geometry ourselves. It requires a new tradition, a new sensitivity, and much learning by everyone.[23]

Intangible design is design in space and time of experience itself. In collaborative design designers and nondesigners participate equally in the process, and contextual design verges on pure art, but with intangible design users' experience becomes the focus of the design process. Objects may be part of an intangible design, but they are secondary to it. Intangible design is particularly relevant to the emerging postindustrial design tasks. Jones writes of the relevance of *Design Methods* to intangible design:

This central new idea of widening the design process means that you don't use the process for the same things as you use the old process for, you don't actually use these new methods for designing buildings. There's very little in that book about designing buildings, it's mainly about designing intangible things. Design an educational system, a traffic system. A traffic system has hardware in it, it has streets and buildings and cars and things, but the essence of it is the movement, which is somewhat intangible. You're designing the movement.[24]

The protagonists of each of these trends have tended to develop methods of design beyond drawing as necessary to suit their individual circumstances. The design tasks undertaken and the methods developed will be investigated in the sections that follow with a view to better understanding the philosophical and methodological basis for these new trends in design; approaches in which the processes of peoples' experience, not physical objects alone, are the motive for design activity.

PART 2
DESIGN TURNED INSIDE OUT

In view of the unsatisfactory nature of much recent design, it is now time to dematerialize our thinking about design, considering first the effects we desire, and then the means through which to achieve them. A wide range of new design approaches, while vastly different in many respects, all reflect the transition from a fixed goal for designing — the production of physical form — to variable ones — designing for different nuances of user experience. In a very real sense these new approaches turn the design process inside out, beginning with an explicit consideration of user behavior and wishes instead of with physical form. This change, this inversion of the aims of designing, has necessitated the development of new methods of design. In the following chapters, approaches to design that focus more directly on use and experience than on physical form will be reviewed with specific attention to the methods through which these designs are realized. A series of cases will be reviewed, each of which reflects a progressive departure from the traditional, geometrically based design-by-drawing process. The work to be reviewed is consistent with John Chris Jones' belief that "the best service, the bravest, is to stop designing, in the ways we do now, and to try for something better. To raise our individual thoughts to the scale of our collective actions. And to give ourselves space to act accordingly."[1]

4. Collaborative Environmental Design

DEFINING COLLABORATIVE DESIGN

Collaborative design is a process through which all of the people affected by designing can become meaningfully involved in the design process. The key to collaborative design approaches, as John Chris Jones pointed out, is that they

... permit collaboration *before* "the concept", the organising idea, the back-of-the envelope-sketch, "the design" has emerged (provided the leading designer knows how to switch from being the person responsible for the result to being the one who ensures that "the process is right"). The new methods, properly used, release everyone from the tyrrany of imposed ideas and enable each to contribute to, and to act upon, the best that everyone is capable of imagining and doing. This is not easy. It requires not only new methods but a new conception of the self.[1]

What Jones envisions is a radical redesign of the design process, a reform in which designers and users are equal partners, not just in shaping the results of designing, but in determining the goals and aims of the design process itself.

The nature, and importance, of collaboration is not limited to producing better design objects. Rather, the intent is to open up designing — to make it a public process. Designers are not eliminated in this transition, but their roles change radically. Instead of simply dictating physical form, they become facilitators, enabling laypeople to collaborate fully in the design process. The merits of user involvement in the design process has been the subject of sometimes fierce debate, particularly in application to environmental design. A number of cases of user involvement in environmental design will now be reviewed to determine the extent to which true collaboration in the design process was realized.

DESIGN PHENOMENA

A precursor to any collaborative environmental design is the realization that the multifaceted phenomena of user experience must guide the development of built form. Henry David Thoreau addressed this point in *Walden:* "What of architectural beauty I now see, I know has grown gradually from within outwards, out of the necessities and character of the indweller."[2] In truly collaborative environmental design the "necessities and character of the indweller" become the basis for production of physical form.

I have developed a system of collaborative environmental design that embodies this idea. With the system, design proceeds from the inside out, beginning with a consideration of user activities and evolving gradually, through use of a kit of modular scale models, into a physical form. The process begins with an interview to determine the clients' particular desires for their space. The interview generally lasts about an hour. After this initial client meeting an analysis of user requirements is generated and large-scale models $(3/4'' = 1' \ 0'')$ of the space, and of the furnishings and equipment specified by the client, are prepared. A second meeting, the design collaboration session, is held a few weeks later in which the clients "act out" each of their daily activities sequentially with a scale human figure, arranging scale furniture and equipment as appropriate to suit the activities. At this stage of the process the designer will suggest some alternative spatial arrangements that might better house the clients' activities and better reflect their wishes for the design. The clients tend to be quite good at expressing their individual design ideas, but are less skilled at making them work together; this is the main contribution that the designer makes during the process. At the conclusion of the session the clients are asked to "perform" each of their daily activities using a scale figure in the model to ensure that the design is satisfactory, making adjustments as necessary. The design collaboration sessions also are about an hour in length.

A videotape of each design collaboration session is made and subsequently analyzed to determine the evolution of the design, identifying the clients' progressive design decisions. Photographs are taken of the final model, and an annotated scale sketch of the model is made, from which final drawings are generated. The model kit is then disassembled and the process can be repeated with other clients.

The modeling system was originally developed by a former professor of mine, Alton J. DeLong, and I have refined and implemented it in a number of different contexts. In one case, I adapted the system for use on a World Bank-initiated squatter settlement project in Amman, Jordan, as a means through which to involve the erstwhile squatters directly in the design of their new houses. Rita Mansur, an architect on the project, observed of her experience with the process, "Most people have a clear idea of what they want and what they need. As an architect, you get a better idea of what they need; for example, the number of rooms and their sizes, using the method."[3]

A more recent, and perhaps more directly relevant, application of the system was to the design of a Conference Headquarters Office for the Indiana University Conference Bureau. The client for the project was Janet Brady James, director of the Conference Bureau, who wished to develop an entirely new space to serve as a well equipped temporary base for visiting conference organizers and their administrative assistants in which both executive meetings and routine

 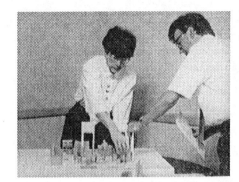

 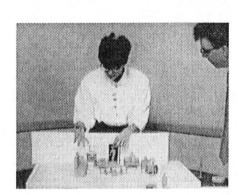

Conference Headquarters Office. Views from video of Design Collaboration Session.
The client is on the left, the collaborating designer on the right.

conference administration could take place. The Conference Headquarters Office was intended to replace the presently unsatisfactory solutions to these needs: the rental of underequipped meeting rooms or hotel suites for use by conference organizers. No location had been allocated to the Conference Headquarters Office at the time of the design collaboration session, but the size of the space was to be approximately 500 square feet. Based on the initial client interview, a series of analyses of the Conference Headquarters Office were carried out. These included the generation of: a user profile, in which the people to use the space were identified; a chronological inventory of activities to take place within the space; and a listing of the desired physical aspects of the space.

The evolution of the design of the Conference Headquarters Office took place during the design collaboration session. The client was asked to "act out" each of the activities that would take place in the space, using scale human figures and whatever model furniture and equipment was needed to complete the activity. Throughout the process the client was free to adjust previous spatial arrangements to accommodate new needs. The collaborating designer also offered suggestions when asked by the client. The design process proceeded very smoothly and within one hour a final design that pleased the client had been generated.

After the design collaboration session the client commented on the design process:

This is the first time I've used a model. I had not approached it with a clear idea of how the furniture would actually be configured to serve these different purposes. It intrigues

Conference Headquarters Office. Digest of Design Evolution.
The steps in the design of the space are set out and are categorized according to the physical features added to the space. A small floor plan of the space during each step is included, as well as client comments (in quotation marks) and/or a commentary on the decisions made during each step.

Step 1: Identify Entry
"It will be important for me to identify the entry as there will be so much traffic coming in and out of the room. We need to identify where the point of passage is."

Step 2: Locate Storage Units and Work Spaces for Use by Conference Helpers
"Traffic will be coming directly to put materials on the surfaces, either to layout and collate them, to staple them, or perhaps to put them in cabinets. There will be stuffed folders for the conference participants, there will be handouts, there might be rosters, abstracts of papers, and instructions for people who will be working in here. So there will be a lot of need for surface area and shelves in here to store things on."

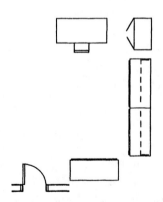

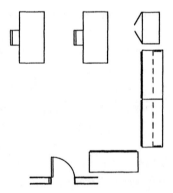

Step 3: Locate Desk for Conference Secretary
"The next thing that people will be looking for is a desk where they can set up new materials. It might be a good idea to have a kind of locker near to the desk so that any kind of clerical supplies, such as those that a secretary might need, will be close to them; that is not necessarily the same as conference-related supplies."

Step 4: Locate Additional Desk
"We would like to have a clerical situation where there is some degree of separation between two potential clerical functions. For example, let's say one person is typing material for the chairperson alone and is not responsible for answering the phone or for generating materials off the computer. At the same time this desk might be used by the chairperson in lieu of this person so it should be situated in such a way that it has some privacy — now that's a trick!"

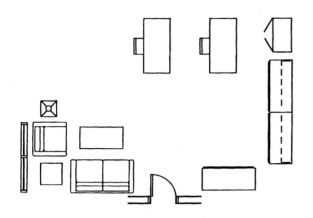

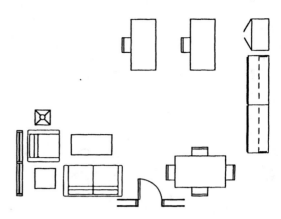

Step 5: Locate Comfortable Seating Area

Client identifies area for conference organizer and administrative assistant to meet on the day before the conference to discuss the status of conference preparations.

"I would put that in a comfortable area. Anything you can do to foster a sense of relaxation and least stress would be desirable on this day — it's a rough day. The clerical and storage areas would be very functional, it is important that they have strong, good light, but in this area we would really like to soften the whole effect, which is why we specified more comfortable upholstered furniture and uplighting, as opposed to the other areas in which we are talking about a much more functional effect."

Step 6: Add Meeting Table

The client's next activity to house was the meeting of the conference's local arrangements committee, for which she chose and located a meeting table.

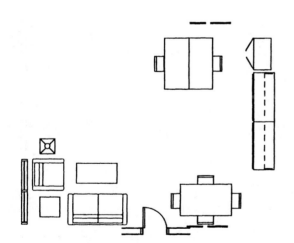

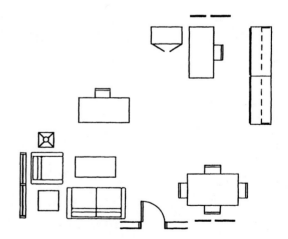

Step 7: Client Rearranges Desks

"Now the model shows our room is getting very crowded. Perhaps the space isn't arranged most efficiently. Perhaps we can arrange this with the desks back to back; that might give us a little more room but of course whoever is working here is not going to be very private."

Client locates map and master conference schedule by conference secretary, and a duplicate set is place where all conference-related supplies are kept.

Step 8: Divide Into Public and Private Zones

Client locates additional desk in front of comfortable seating area creating a more private zone, separated from the room's more public functions, and makes other minor adjustments to the space.

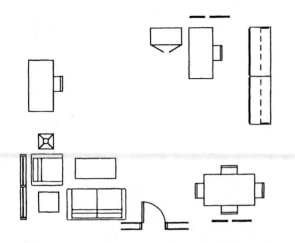

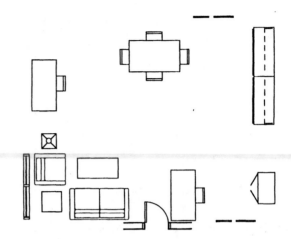

Step 9: Differentiate Private Zones

Client rearranges private zone to provide a more informal area for interviews and relaxation and a more formal area for work.

"I think this looks a little awkward to have a desk immediately facing the sitting area so it may be that we do something that is not quite so hemmed in. I think there needs to be a sense of openness and flow in order to keep the perception of chaos at a minimum. I think adding a window in the private area would be an enhancement, while in the public area it would be a distraction."

Step 10: Relocate Conference Secretary's Desk and Meeting Table

"People expect to be helped as soon as they step through the threshold, having somebody there by the door instead of having to call across the room. Also with this arrangement people using the meeting table are less likely to be disturbed."

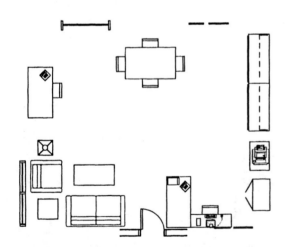

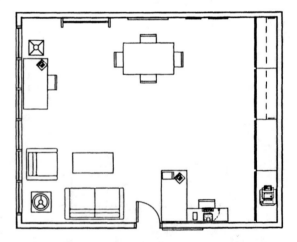

Step 11: Define Layout of Office Equipment

The conference secretary is given a computer and modem to be placed on a typing return, with a laserprinter behind the desk, as well as a telephone and answering machine. A telephone is also placed on the desk in the private zone. A coat rack is added.

Step 12: Add Walls, Details, and Make Revisions to Space

"I'm not completely happy with this tall storage cabinet because it seems to be a bit claustrophobic. It's very tight — I think it's because this cabinet overshadows all the things here so instead of having a tall one we could do with a shorter one."

Bulletin boards are located outside by the entry and inside the space. The desk area in the private zone seems underdeveloped and the client suggests ways of improving it.

"Give this person a window, which makes it more pleasant. You might give them a standing light and you could use a more 'executive' type desk chair."

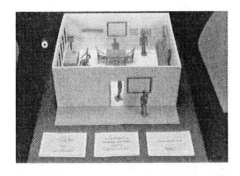

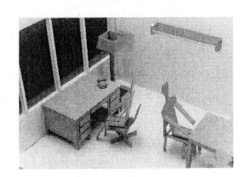

**Conference
Headquarters Office.
Views of final model.**

me that the process made it apparent that the original layout [I had in mind] was not conducive to the kind of thing we wanted so I enjoyed it, it was a nice experience. I like the model system. Particularly if you have multiple uses for a room, going through this exercise is very useful.[4]

As reflected by the client's comments, use of the modeling system is an effective means through which nondesigners can collaborate in the design process. It is especially useful in application to complex, multiuse spaces, such as the Conference Headquarters Office, in which the use of the space changes frequently over time. Effective user involvement in design leads not only to better adapted spaces but also to more satisfied users. People enjoy the process, especially the opportunity to "have their say" about the environments in which they will have to live or work.

Along with the many benefits of the system, there are a number of limitations that must be noted. The principal one is the scale of task that can be undertaken using the system. Because of the scale (and size) of the modeling apparatus, large-scale design tasks cannot easily be undertaken; 1,250 square feet is about the maximum area that can be designed at any one time. In addition, the maximum number of clients or user representatives who can work on the model simultaneously are effectively limited to two or three. While the use of the modeling system helps address the use of a space, it is not very effective in dealing with larger-scale architectural issues, such as defining structural systems, or the external appearance and detailing of a space. Architectural services such as the production of working drawings and specifications are still required for the outcomes of the collaboration sessions to be realized in built form.

One additional, important point is that nondesigners seem able to participate effectively in the design process through use of modular scale models when the task is one of limited scale with which they are very familiar. In my experience in Jordan, for example, the project beneficiaries were very articulate about their wishes for their future houses, and were able to demonstrate their needs directly through use of the model kits. Similarly, the client for the Conference Headquarters Office had identified a need for a space that did not presently exist and she was very clear about what the requirements for such a space were. Through the model kit she too was able, in collaboration with a designer, to generate a design to house the activities that she had specified. Often, however, laypeople find it very difficult to collaborate in the design of something with which they are not very familiar. In the Jordan case, for example, a husband tried to design his future house without permitting his wife to have any input. It quickly became apparent that he was involved in very few of the activities in the house. When unable to generate a design he reluctantly asked his wife to "help," and a design that pleased them both was then quickly generated.

Through the use of modular scale models, I have been able to help nondesigners collaborate in the environmental design process, producing designs that derive directly from their activities, needs, and wishes. What I have *not* done, however, is provide a workable alternative to present-day architectural design methods. As the scale, complexity, and number of people affected by design increases, it becomes ever more difficult to realize effective user involvement in the environmental design process. Some practitioners have, however, attempted to do so, and their efforts will now be reviewed.

USER INVOLVEMENT IN ARCHITECTURAL DESIGN

Despite the difficulties involved, a number of architects have attempted to involve the eventual end users of their buildings in the design process. Among the most notable, and reported, of these experiments are Ralph Erskine's Byker project in Newcastle, England; Lucien Kroll's medical faculty buildings at the University of Louvain, Belgium; and Christopher Alexander's numerous applications, with his team from the Center for Environmental Structure, of the pattern language. In each of these cases different approaches to user involvement were chosen.

Ralph Erskine, the British-born, Swedish-based architect, was hired in 1969 by the Newcastle town council to come up with a plan for the redevelopment of

**Ralph Erskine.
Byker Project,
Newcastle, 1974.**
A view of a public
courtyard.

the run-down Byker area of the city. The Byker Project was a mammoth undertaking in which more than 10,000 residents were to be resettled on a 200-acre site. Erskine was hired on the basis of his reputation as "the humane architect."[5] The key concept of Erskine's plan for Byker was that the area residents should participate directly in shaping the new design. To help realize this, Erskine established a storefront office on the project site to which local residents were invited to come and give their opinions on the area's redevelopment.

Erskine's intention in the design of the Project was, as Colin Amery put it, "to initiate a large degree of participation."[6] But, as Amery points out:

It was soon learned by the architects that it is a task to make three-dimensional design comprehensible. There is a real dilemma inherent in participatory designing. The resi-

**Ralph Erskine.
Byker Project,
Newcastle, 1974.**
A view of the inward-
facing side of the
Byker wall.

Ralph Erskine. Byker Project, Newcastle, 1974. A view of the outward-facing side of the massive "Byker Wall," which was, despite the pretense of participation, "the architect's imposed solution."

dents have absolutely no control over any redevelopment and they lack skills to actually design and build their own houses. What is happening in Byker is a middle way. Everyone is consulted so misconceptions and rumours are dispelled at an early stage — but the people who benefit from the lengthy consultations are not those who take part but those who come after them.[7]

So despite their initial intentions, Erskine and his design team used a fairly traditional design process; some users were consulted, but there was no direct user participation in designing. The unsatisfactory nature of this cursory consultation is recounted by Peter Malpass:

Meetings with tenants were held throughout the design stage and while the houses were being built they eagerly monitored progress and generally kept an eye on the builders. When the houses were finished, in mid-1971, at first the tenants were euphoric. But soon problems began to emerge and there followed a lengthy dialogue, even wrangle, between them, the architects and the Housing Department. Less than a year after they moved in the residents formed a Tenants Association through which to pursue their grievances with the corporation and at least for a time some success was achieved, despite attempts to write off the complaints as petty.[8]

Having failed to initiate an effective process of participation, Erskine fell back on his architectural training and focused on the production of form. This is affirmed by Colin Amery, in an absurd but truthful revelation of the negligible role of user involvement in the Byker scheme:

The great perimeter block is, despite all the public participation, the architect's imposed design solution. It could turn out to be a great success, it could equally become a vandalised dwelling block. As a housing scheme it is dangerously willful, as an architectural form-maker's contribution to a townscape dream it is undeniably impressive. It stands as a built statement to prove the architects know best and it is a contradiction of the doctrines preached by the architect.[9]

Lucien Kroll.
**Medical Faculty Buildings,
Woluwé-St. Lambert,
Belgium.
Exterior views.**
These images illustrate
tghe "rich and intricate
forms" that resulted from
Kroll's participatory
design process.

Lucien Kroll, in contrast to Erskine, was much more ambitious in his attempt to involve prospective users in the design of the medical faculty buildings at the University of Louvain. Charles Jencks described the process Kroll followed:

Kroll and his team . . . really involved a community (or part of it) in design decisions. The students, who were divided into flexible teams, participated in designing the buildings along with Kroll, who acted rather like an orchestra leader. They shifted small bits of plastic foam around in working out the overall model. When disputes arose, or one group became too dogmatic and fixed, Kroll reorganized the teams so that each one became familiar with each other's problems, until a possible solution was in sight. Not until then did he draw up the plans and sections which made it workable. The resultant buildings show a complexity and richness of meaning, a delicate pluralism, that usually takes years to achieve and is the result of many inhabitants making small adjustments over time.[10]

Here we see Kroll changing the design process from one of simple consultation to one of active participation. Kroll set out his philosophy of design in an article titled "Soft Zone":

Generally, architects are the sole masters in their specialty and consequently believe that they know enough about this subject and absorb themselves in fashioning and embellishing the "architectural object" without imagining the behaviour this will impose on its inhabitants and without experiencing, even through study groups, the unanimities, the contradictions, the incompatibilities from which a complex *milieu* is woven.[11]

As an alternative to traditional design approaches that effectively ignore user behavior, Kroll recognized the need for and importance of user participation in design, introducing his modular modeling system to better enable laypeople to become involved in the design process.

Not surprisingly, with his rejection of the "architect knows best" philosophy, Kroll and his work have received a great deal of criticism. Geoffrey Broadbent, for example, writes that the net result of user participation in the design of the buildings at Louvain is

. . . gross discomfort for those who have to use these buildings. Yet the rich and intricate forms in which they are conceived could have been turned by Kroll himself to maximum environmental advantage — *if* he had possessed, and insisted on exercising, the necessary expertise. Instead of that, his insistence on total participation — for the best of possible motives — has resulted, sadly, in buildings which are *less* acceptable to their users than they could have been if a well informed architect had exercised his personal skill![12]

Broadbent's comments must be interpreted in terms of his belief that design professionals are uniquely qualified to shape the built environment. He has written:

Like all professionals, architects and planners have particular responsibilities. Our job is to look at humanity, to look at the environment in which humanity finds itself, and to find ways of reconciling the two. By becoming architects we have chosen to affect this reconciliation between the needs of those people and the environment through the medium of making buildings.[13]

In contrast, the designer who seeks to bring about meaningful user involvement in the design process must undergo a change of role and self-image. This change is not an abdication of responsibility, but a change from actively to passively shaping the outcomes of designing. Kroll, for example, defined a structural grid and then initiated the participatory process that determined the overall building shape. In his work we see an increasing focus on the process and effects of design, with less emphasis on the properties of the designed object. It may be true that Kroll's building wasn't fully successful from the users' point of view, as Broadbent suggests, but this perceived failure is not intrinsic to user involvement in design, as he also seems to imply.

Christopher Alexander, for example, has sought to embody the expertise that Broadbent claims is required for design in his pattern language. Alexander observes that through use of a pattern language people, any people, can understand and effectively participate in a design process:

84

A person with a pattern language can design any part of the environment. He does not need to be an "expert." The expertise is in the language. He can equally well contribute to the planning of a city, design his own house, or remodel a single room, because in each case he knows the relevant patterns, knows how to combine them, and knows how the particular piece he is working on fits into the larger whole.[14]

Alexander and his team have applied the pattern language to a wide variety of tasks, including clusters of low-cost, self-built houses in Peru and Mexico, a café in Austria, a college campus in Japan, and a number of offices and single-family dwellings in the United States.

Most so-called "design participation" schemes that have been reported in the literature consist simply of, as Charles Jencks notes, "one-sided consultation with those being designed for: they could see the plans beforehand, but didn't have the expertise or power to propose viable alternatives."[15] Such was the case with Ralph Erskine's Byker project. True collaborative environmental design, on the other hand, necessitates a fundamental change in the design process, and in designers' roles within it. Instead of imposing a formal solution, the designer in a collaborative process sets up the circumstances, for example through the use of models or a language, through which nondesigners are able to participate directly in the design process. It is essential, as John Chris Jones points out, that user involvement take place *before*, not after, concept fixing, even in sketch form, takes place. To a greater or lesser extent this was the case in my applications of modular scale models, and in Kroll's, as well as in the work of Alexander's team.

CHANGING ROLES, CHANGING AIMS

The importance, the necessity, of user involvement in architectural design is clearly set out by Christopher Alexander: "It is essential that the people of a society, together, all the millions of them, not just professional architects, design all the millions of places. There is no other way that human variety, and the reality of specific human lives, can find their way into the structure of the places."[16] But, as John Chris Jones points out, "To share the design process with users is not as easy as it sounds. It needs a change of roles, of self-images, on both sides."[17]

It is precisely this changing of roles that is an essential precursor to any collaborative designing. Jones develops this thought by further noting:

As larger groups begin to work together in design, we need not only looser roles but more public ways of thinking aloud. More visible design processes so that everyone can see what is being decided, and why, *before*, not after, the main decisions are made. Collaboration before concept-fixing is perhaps the main strength of the new design methods. The other strength is to provide means of *un*learning, publicly, with changing, not fixed, self-images.[18]

As designers make this transition, the aims and purposes of designing themselves change. In the case of successful collaborative environmental design, the principal focus of designing is on user experience and the process of collaboration itself is seen to have value. Put another way, with collaborative design the "software" aspects of environments — use, perception, and experience — take precedence over the "hardware" aspect — physical form.

The experience of collaboration, and the attention to people's activities, wishes, and desires, suggest new dimensions of designing, many of which are independent of physical form altogether. This seemingly radical notion is termed "contextual design" by Jones. Contextual design represents an attempt to design explicitly for user perception and experience; the means chosen for designing depending on the experience sought. This approach to designing will be examined in detail in the following chapter.

5. Contextual Design

Most collaborative design approaches were initiated in an attempt to shape form in a way that more closely fitted the requirements and desires of users. A beneficial by-product of collaborative designing was the emotional and psychological satisfaction felt by those participating in the process. With contextual design, however, the design process is redirected from a fixed aim — the production of physical form — to variable aims — the tailoring of design to explicitly, rather than implicitly, address user perception. John Chris Jones, referring to this transition, noted that what is needed in design is "a change *from* the specifying of geometry, physical form, *to* the making of a context, a situation."[1] The reasons for this transition away from an object fixation in design are, paradoxically perhaps, addressed by the man who is widely credited to be the founder of postmodernism, Robert Venturi. Recall that he and his coauthors wrote:

This is not the time and ours is not the environment for heroic communication through pure architecture. Each medium has its day, and the rhetorical environmental statements of our time — civic, commercial, or residential — will come from media more purely symbolic, perhaps less static and more adaptable to the scale of our environment.[2]

The more purely symbolic, less static, and more adaptable media Venturi and his coauthors mention are the subjects of contextual designing.

The seeds of contextual design were present when John Chris Jones wrote in the late 1950s:

In endeavouring to design things that will not harmfully disturb the user's mind the designer will find himself measuring and taking account of each and every effect that the environment can have on the senses. Pattern, texture, absorption and reflection of heat or sound, smell, psychological effects of enclosure, exposure and every intermediate stage, all these and many more would be considered and allowed for in the design of every part of every article or building.[3]

One recent design approach that has sought explicitly to address the perceptual effects of designing is variously termed *design primario*, *primary design*, and *soft design*. This approach was developed by Italian color consultant Clino Trini Castelli, who has applied his ideas in work for, among others, Fiat, Olivetti, and

Herman Miller. John Thackara addresses Castelli's design philosophy in his article "Designing without Form":

Clino Castelli's *design primario* concept tackles the non-material, subjective, "soft" aspects of environmental design. As he explains: "the softer elements, and the more subjective uses of design, have largely been ignored in recent years. The ways in which light, colour, and texture affect our perceptions, our deepest feelings about an object or a place, do belong in the province of design, but are uncharted territory". Castelli's *design primario* programme aims to develop an understanding of how subjective perception affects the quality of an object or an environment, and then to apply this knowledge to problems of design and production. "Ideally," Castelli says, "my approach to design would involve the elimination of form altogether — designing only with light, sound, texture, and so on".[4]

Julian Gibb also addresses this approach in an article titled "Soft: An Appeal to Common Senses":

Primary Design is defined as the tools and concepts required for dealing with the sensory constituents of reality, a system of countermeasures employed to offset the growing influence of technology in our society . . . to compensate for the inhuman, alienating aspects of technology which inform first, the majority of the functional objects produced by mass production methods, and second, many workplaces in the electronic age. . . .

The important keyword is Soft. Soft is a bridge between mechanism and organism, between artificial, mechanical order and natural variety. Castelli argues that because architectural and product design is still essentially executed through the medium of two-dimensional graphic representation, the "objective" properties of a product tend to be stressed at the expense of the subjective aspect, including sensual qualities. Castelli stresses that "today it is increasingly the subjective aspects, the Soft aspects of the product, that connote and define a new concept of quality".[5]

Andrea Branzi charted the development of primary design and its focus on the soft aspects of the environment:

The starting point for primary design was this: industrial design, as part of the Modern Movement, and indeed the whole ideology of design, is based on the conviction that the fundamental quality of a setting or an object lies in the correctness of its structure, i.e. the balanced harmony of form, structure and functional requirements; from this equilibrium derives, in a direct and almost mechanical manner, the expressiveness of the product, its social value, and in the case of architecture its fitness for habitation, i.e. the quality of its domestic space. The origins of this conviction lie far back in time. "Design primario" stood aside from this tradition, shifting attention onto other structural qualities, which we called "soft"; to the way of thinking of both the Modern Movement and classical architecture, these were generally wholly secondary, and included colour, light, micro-climate, decoration and even odours and background music. These are all experiences of space that are not directly assimilable to the constituent qualities of an environment or an object, but are linked instead with the physical perception of space, i.e. with its "bodily" consumption. In this way new attention was paid to the user's real sensitivity of perception, bound up more closely with the direct consumption of soft structure than with the grasping of an architectural composition and its sophisticated allegories of form. . . .

To some extent this type of experience harks back to a conception of architectural space predating the Renaissance. The Romanesque cathedral, for example, cannot be perceived in isolation from several factors that are apparently subsidiary but in reality [are] fundamental to the perception of its significance: these include sudden changes in temperature between interior and exterior, the nature of the acoustics, the highly unusual lighting that filters through panes of stained glass and even the smell of the unventilated building, heightened by candles and incense. The whole of this complex of soft structures forms an integral part of the definition of this type of monument, not only in its everyday experience but also in the monumental entity's complexity of expression. This sort of directly physical experience of architectural space was completely abandoned in the revolution of the Renaissance, which shifted the relations with the human body from the direct sphere of the senses to that of proportions; architecture moved towards an exclusively ideological definition, whose perception is based on a philosophical concept, that is to say a form of thought that is physically realized in space.[6]

The transition in architecture from a focus on the senses to a preoccupation with proportions that took place in the Renaissance was accompanied by a shift in methods from master builders who worked on site to the use of design-by-drawing in which the planning of an object or environment was, for the first time, separated from the contexts of making and use. In order to recover the sensory responsiveness of pre-Renaissance architecture, the use of design-by-drawing must be rejected and new methods substituted in its place. As Branzi writes:

To design colours, lights and decorations, instruments different from the traditional architectural ones of pencil, square and compass were required. To register and control this kind of parameter, other working instruments were indispensable. "Design primario" was also concerned with the invention of new instruments, which had to be worked out in advance and to contain preselected information; in other words they had to be open structures within which individual designers or users could proceed further.[7]

Castelli's experiments with primary design notwithstanding, the concept of contextual design in practice is still underdeveloped. These ideas have been much more thoroughly explored by some artists whose work is explicitly intended as a catalyst to perceptual experience. The artists whose work seem to best embody this perceptual orientation — albeit in rather different ways — are Robert Wilson in his theater pieces, Christo in his projects, and Brian Eno in his ambient music, videos, and installations. Each of these artists has a background in architecture, design, or fine art, but all have rejected traditional, object-oriented art in favor of more perceptually oriented approaches.

ROBERT WILSON'S NONNARRATIVE THEATER

One of the most striking theater pieces I have seen was *the Knee Plays* for Robert Wilson's opera *the CIVIL warS: a tree is best measured when it is down*. The thirteen individual Knee Plays were originally developed to serve as segues between the different parts of the opera. *The CIVIL warS* itself was to be global in scale, tak-

Portrait of Robert Wilson.

ing place over the course of twelve continuous hours with the individual sections being performed in six different countries. Performances of the opera were to be broadcast by satellite as part of the Olympic Arts Festival held in association with the 1984 Summer Olympics in Los Angeles but, due to a lack of funding, presentation of the complete *CIVIL warS* was canceled. The individual sections, however, had already been developed, and *the Knee Plays* have been performed individually.

Wilson's work has been variously described as "hypnotic," "beautiful," and "boring," owing to the frequently long duration of his pieces and his greater emphasis on stage settings and music than on text and action. *The Knee Plays* was slightly different in that it was very concise, lasting less than an hour, and very lively, thanks in large part to a musical score by David Byrne, which was performed by a brass band and punctuated by quirky, non sequitur narration. The "story," such as it is, is subservient to Wilson's wide-ranging visual imagery. The experience of *the Knee Plays* is a rich one. In addition to Byrne's music, there is an almost continuous flow of nontraditional dance throughout the piece. The central focus, however, is on the ever-evolving, metaphorically evocative, but essentially nonnaturalistic stage sets and lighting. One reviewer, John Howell of *Artforum*, wrote:

The Knee Plays, a collaborative mixed media opera, almost effortlessly achieved the kind of successful melding of theatrical elements that most other such performances strain for . . . Wilson's principal conceit, that of putting forward the usually secondary elements of theater — lighting, decor, props — as the principal subject of his dramas, continued as *the Knee Play* modus operandi. Developed from his architectonic drawings, the playlets' central "characters" were the toylike objects on stage; principle among these were a tree, a boat, a bird, and a puppet. The "story" was the unfolding of their multiple physical transformations accomplished by a squad of stagehand-like performers.[8]

Knee Play 1

A man in a tree is sleeping.
A lion is beneath the tree.
Silence.
The man climbs down the tree, but is chased
back up by the lion.
The man settles in the tree to read a book.

**Robert Wilson.
Sketch and Performance
View of Knee Play 1.
From the *Knee Plays* by
Robert Wilson and David
Byrne from the *CIVIL
warS: a tree is best
measured when it is
down* by Robert Wilson.
Sketches with text, such
as this, are used as the
basis for the collabora-
tive process of generat-
ing Wilson's theater
pieces. In the perfor-
mance illustrated, which
took place at the Walker
Art Center, the stage orientation was reversed.**

Addressing the perceptual effect of Wilson's work, Howell observed:

Some scenes were so transcendent within their short time spans that a consciousness-
expanding dreaminess took over. When a large wooden bird "flew" across the stage to
Byrne's Brian Eno-esque sonic wash, when the rear backdrop filled up with brilliantly
colored whirls of biomorphic shapes, when dancers "swam" through cinematic waves,
the Knee Plays became a transporting spectacle of associative meanings. No performance
artist is so adept at creating such moods as Wilson, and those of *the Knee Plays* were particularly evocative. Because these evanescent impressions were the result of a carefully
calibrated inter-weaving of music, movement, design, and text, with a logical subtext
that provided a sturdy ideational skeleton for their seductive flesh, they were not *just*
beautiful.[9]

Wilson's work is often termed "nonnarrative theater" because his focus is on
creating perceptual effects, not communicating a predetermined "meaning."
Janny Donker, who chronicled the evolution of the opera, addresses this point:
"one can hardly expect to be able to distill from *the CIVIL warS* something like a
plot, a coherent narrative that can be told or re-told apart from seeing the performance. Nothing of the sort is likely to appear even when the opera will be
completed."[10]

This aspect of Wilson's work has remained constant from his early pieces,
such as *KA MOUNTAIN AND GUARDenia TERRACE*, which lasted seven days
and seven nights and which was "staged" on the side of a mountain in Iran in
1972, through to the present day. Among his other major nonnarrative theater

pieces are *Deafman Glance* (1970), *The Life and Times of Joseph Stalin* (1973), *A Letter for Queen Victoria* (1974), *I Was Sitting on My Patio This Guy Appeared I Thought I Was Hallucinating* (1977), and *Death, Destruction and Detroit* (1979). Wilson is probably best known, however, for his collaboration with composer Philip Glass on the opera, or "music theater" piece, *Einstein on the Beach*, which was originally performed in 1976.

The effect of the nonnarrative approach to theater is addressed by two of Wilson's collaborators. Donker writes:

Hans-Peter Kuhn relates how a woman in Berlin, after seeing Wilson's *Death, Destruction and Detroit*, declared her inability to tell what it was about, "but never before learned so much about myself in the theatre." And Sheryl Sutton: The important thing is what happens to you when you sit watching, completely relaxed. It's our task as actors to enable you to relax. Only if we don't try to force something upon the audience, it becomes possible for you to get from the play whatever it happens to contain for you. We are there and not there at the same time.[11]

Wilson's educational background, interestingly, is in architecture, not theater or fine art. He studied architecture at Pratt Institute and apprenticed with architect Paolo Soleri. Upon his arrival in New York from his home in Waco, Texas, he was soon drawn to experimental theater. Addressing Wilson's role in his theater pieces, Dale Harris writes: "Today, acting as a director-playwright, he decides on the characters, the action, and the style of his pieces. Since he neither composes music nor choreographs, his is a collaborative art, the purpose of this collaboration being to give his original conception a vivid theatrical identity."[12] Similarly, David Byrne, who wrote the score for *the Knee Plays*, studied at the Rhode Island School of Design before starting the acclaimed new-wave rock group Talking Heads. Byrne is now known not only for his fusion of diverse musical styles, but also for his innovative graphic, video, and film work.

If the key to architecture is the arrangement of space, then the key to Wilson's work, since he abandoned architecture, is the manipulation and arrangement — the sculpting — of time. In fact, time is the dimension by which Wilson's work may best be measured: its manipulation is its meaning. In an article titled "Robert Wilson: It's About Time," Franco Quadri writes:

Wilson divides space into moments, not segments, and the length of the stage can be measured in hours rather than feet. Yes, there is an image, but it must be lighted by time in order for it to be perceived. Time is presented to the spectator as a key for entering Wilson's theater. Through sheer physical effort, one moves beyond the passive contemplation of an image, beyond the estheticizing charm of his friezes. Wilson's performances are abnormally long — from 7 hours, to 12 hours, to 24 hours, to 7 days and 7 nights; the first part of his most recent work, *the CIVIL warS: a tree is best measured when it is down* (excerpts of which have been shown throughout Europe in 1983 and 1984), extends for 9 hours. This introduces a rhythm different from the usual one of life, thanks to the extension of gesture. This rhythm conquers the spectators' resistance, making them share the rarefied tempo of the actors. When the experience is drawn out to as much as 24 hours, the audience shares the actors' unedited reactions (as in *Overture,* when in the hours approaching daybreak sleep created an unforeseen syntony between actors and audience).

. . ."the Project" in all its technical organizational elaborations — becomes in itself an integral part of the expression (like the endless studies that precede Christo's actual interventions). It is like the grand construction projects of ages past, when the cathedrals were built thanks to collective contributions from wide-ranging sources over long periods of time — the individual pieces meticulously fitted together here by the demiurgics of Robert Wilson, architect of time.[13]

Similarly John Howell writes, "Wilson has created several major operatic works in European theaters, and has developed the latent subject of his earlier works — light, from its literal effects to its transcendental — into his chief theatrical subject: time."[14]

In viewing *the Knee Plays* I felt a sort of visceral involvement that was relaxing and engaging at the same time, very much like the feeling I have when meditating or practicing yoga. Addressing this effect in one of Wilson's other works, Melissa Harris writes:

Much of the criticism of *Einstein on the Beach* finds fault with its hypnotic qualities, stating that the viewer must give him/herself up to the piece in a trance-like surrender: it becomes meditative, and in this way escapist, theater. I disagree. Rather than passifying its audience, *Einstein on the Beach* demands a high state of consciousness and induces an

Knee Play 5

The boat is beached on rocks.
Three people write graffiti on it.

Robert Wilson. Drawing and Sketch for Knee Play 5. From the *Knee Plays* by Robert Wilson and David Byrne from the *CIVIL warS: a tree is best measured when it is down* by Robert Wilson. The production of graphite drawings precedes the generation of sketches and the drafting of the "storyline" for Wilson's plays.

Robert Wilson.
Drawing, Sketch,
and Performance View
of Knee Play 6.
From the *Knee Plays* by
Robert Wilson and David
Byrne from the *CIVIL
warS: a tree is best
measured when it is
down* by Robert Wilson.
Here is a complete
sequence of Wilson's
theatrical images, begin-
ning with a graphite
drawing, from which a
sketch and text are
derived, and concluding
with a view from a per-
formance at the Walker
Art Center in which the
stage orientation was
reversed.

Knee Play 6

The boat sails along a coast.
On shore, two people load a cannon and fire
at the boat.
The boat is hit and breaks up.
The hull sinks and the cain floats on.

alertness to every detail, no matter how obscure. Certainly, the opera's talismanic aura is
spellbinding, but not subliminally.[15]

The criticism of Wilson's work that Harris cites and rightly rebuts is also
directed, equally wrongly, to the work of Brian Eno, to be reviewed subsequently.

Wilson begins the planning of his theater pieces by drawing, working freely in graphite on paper. He creates scores of expressionistic drawings, from which scenes gradually take shape. Once refined, Wilson arranges these drawings in a visually pleasing sequence and only then does he begin to evolve a "story" or structure to accompany the scenes he has drawn; only then do they become, effectively, storyboards from which the remainder of the production evolves. Dale Harris describes this process:

As the sketches for one of his projects multiply, Wilson begins to find interesting relationships between them, and thus levels of meaning of which he had not at first been aware. By pinning up the drawings in various sequences on the . . . blank walls of his apartment, he can see whole sections of the work at a single glance. From beginning to end his concepts remain essentially visual.[16]

David Byrne used a very similar process when composing his film *True Stories*. He wrote in his book on the film:

The way this film framework was constructed was inspired a little bit by my work with Robert Wilson, by his working process. He often begins work on a theatre piece with mainly visual ideas and then layers the sound and dialogue on top of that. I used a similar method. I covered the wall with drawings, most of them representing events that could take place in one town. Then I reordered the drawings, again and again, until they seemed to have some sort of flow. Meanwhile I assigned the characters inspired by the tabloid newspaper articles to the people represented in the drawings . . . I had ordered a series of dramatic events and songs, represented by the drawings on the wall.[17]

Wilson makes no explicit attempt to synchronize the changes in sets, text, stage action, and music produced by his various collaborators to one another. As in the collaborations between avant-garde choreographer Merce Cunningham and composer John Cage in which the dance sequences and the music are developed completely independently, Wilson leaves the synthesis of ideas, the creation of "meaning," to the audience, as individuals. He does not attempt to dictate or impose any meaning. Jill Johnston addressed this point:

Just a cursory reading of the literature about Robert Wilson's work, along with remarks by Wilson himself, reveals one striking, ever repeated, disclaimer: he doesn't mean anything by it. . . . His own remarks about "meaning" focus on a differently expressed abdication of responsibility. He has said repeatedly that he likes to leave things up to the audience. "The audience is free to draw its own conclusions, we don't do that for them." In other words, there are many possible meanings, and you are free to choose or construe your own.[18]

Reflecting back on the field of architecture after his move into theater, Wilson wrote:

It seems that there is still too much concern about building needless monuments. In terms of global planning, cities are still too one- and two-dimensional instead of being three-dimensional. Cities begin to break down because, for example, you can't get from the Empire State Building to the World Trade Center without terrible problems. Part of the problem comes from the architecture schools. When I was in school, a senior project was to design an office tower — that type of approach to design does not help the situation.[19]

Wilson relates an early conceptual alternative he considered:

When I studied architecture, my graduating thesis consisted of an apple. Inside of this apple was a crystal cube which [represented] a window on the world, or TV, or creativity. This model was similar to a medieval city, where the center of the village is the center of cultural life. That can be the theater too.[20]

When asked his views on the Staatsgalerie addition in Stuttgart then recently completed by the late Scottish architect James Stirling, Wilson replied:

It's beautiful but I always think, "So what?" It is good to have attractive monuments, but they still don't solve the problem of the cube in the apple. Cultural centers don't necessarily have to be within marble palaces, they can be anywhere. Something like the Centre Pompidou in Paris is headed in a more interesting direction. It is more like a medieval city, or the center of a village. It is a tourist attraction and may not be the ideal place to contemplate art, but it is still representative of an attitude, a cultural policy lacking in America. My first works were produced by the Pompidou Center, as were my first video tapes. People congregate there. It's a meeting place instead of being a morgue or a museum just collecting the works of dead people. It's also a working place: I worked there with a physicist from Milan and a sound engineer from Berlin, developing "the CIVIL warS." That's more the direction I would like to see architecture or museums take: the Centre Pompidou is a true center, a meeting place where things can happen.[21]

Wilson's work is especially interesting because he has studied, and rejected, architecture, with its focus on space, for theater and its preoccupation with time. Instead of creating more "needless monuments," he has chosen to work in a more dynamic, multisensory way. Through his nonnarrative theater pieces Wilson explictly sets out to create contexts for heightened perceptual experience. His use of the formal aspects of his work as a vehicle, a means to perception, instead of as ends in themselves, exemplifies a rejection of the object orientation in design for a more contextual approach.

CHRISTO'S PROJECTS

I have long admired the work of artist Christo, but nothing in reading about his work, or even seeing his collages, models, and objects in museums, prepared me for the experience of seeing one of his large-scale works installed. I was walking along the right bank of the Seine in Paris one night in the autumn of 1985 when, approaching a bridge, I stepped on what I thought was a drop cloth. It seemed strange that a stone bridge would need to be painted, so I continued up the street, looked back at the bridge, and saw that the entire illuminated bridge had been wrapped in a sandy-colored cloth. I recognized this to be the realization of Christo's *Pont-Neuf Wrapped* project, a model of which I had seen

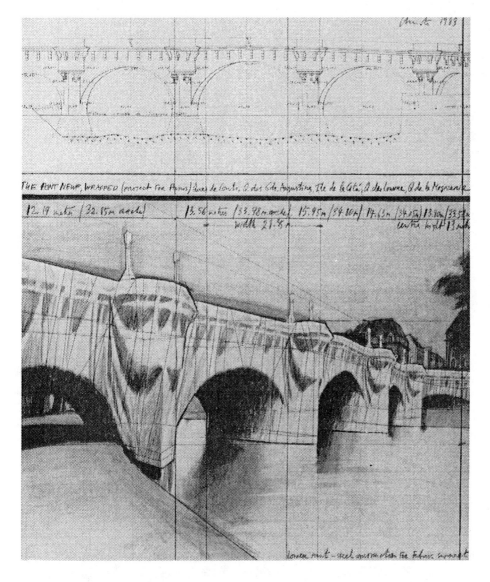

Christo.
The Pont-Neuf
Wrapped, Project
for Paris.
Collage in 2 parts, 1983.
Presentations such as
this are used by Christo
to visualize his projects
and to work out techni-
cal details. They are
then sold to finance
the projects.

just the day before in a museum. The project was the culmination of ten years of effort, though the actual wrapping of the bridge was to last only two weeks.

Christo is renowned for his attention to detail and this was clearly evident in the experience of viewing the *Pont-Neuf Wrapped*. People crossing the bridge were approached by monitors who handed out flyers on the project, in French and English, and small samples of the cloth used in the wrapping. All pedestrian walkways were covered in cloth, but motor traffic continued over the bridge. (It was a condition of the project that during its assembly, presence, and disassembly, all traffic, by foot, road, or water, be able to proceed undisturbed.) My most pleasant discovery came when sitting on the stone seats on the bridge, which had apparently been padded with foam underneath the wrapping, thus further heightening the softening effect of the project.

The installation of the project, which was completed on 22 September 1985, took 7 days and involved 300 professional workers, including engineers, construction workers, scuba divers, and rock climbers. The wrapping of the bridge

**Christo.
The Pont-Neuf
Wrapped, Project
for Paris, 1975–85.**
In this view of the project
in place, a key constraint
that Christo had to com-
ply with is evident — all
traffic, whether by foot,
road, or river, had to
proceed unimpeded
during the project's
assembly, presence,
and disassembly.

required 440,000 square feet of fabric restrained by 42,900 feet of rope. The rope in turn was secured by 12.1 tons of steel chain that encircled the base of each of the bridge's towers, three feet underwater. The project cost $4 million, all of which was paid by Christo through the sale of preparatory drawings, collages, and earlier works. The project was disassembled on 7 October 1985.

Christo's purpose for wrapping the Pont-Neuf is set out in the press release for the project:

Begun under Henri III, the Pont-Neuf was completed in July 1606, during the reign of Henry IV. No other bridge in Paris offers such topographical and visual variety, today as in the past. From 1578 to 1890, the Pont-Neuf underwent continual changes and additions of the most extravagant sort, such as the construction of shops on the bridge under Soufflot, the building, demolition, rebuilding and once again demolition of the massive rococo structure which housed the Samaritaine's water pump. Wrapping the Pont-Neuf continues this tradition of successive metamorphoses by a new sculptural dimension and transforms it, for fourteen days, into a work of art itself. Ropes hold down the fabric to the bridge's surface and maintain the principal shapes, accentuating relief while emphasizing proportions and details of the Pont-Neuf which joins the left and right banks and the Ile de la Cité, the heart of Paris for over two thousand years.[22]

The reaction to the *Pont-Neuf Wrapped* was, once realized, overwhelmingly positive. Though I was set to leave Paris early on the morning after chancing upon it, I rose earlier still to have a second experience of the project as the sun came up. Already there were many people loitering all around the bridge, many of whom were sketching, photographing, or just looking at the wrapped bridge from every possible angle. It is estimated that three million people turned out to see the *Pont-Neuf Wrapped* during the fortnight it was in place.

Critics seemed, on this rare occasion, to speak almost with one voice. Char-

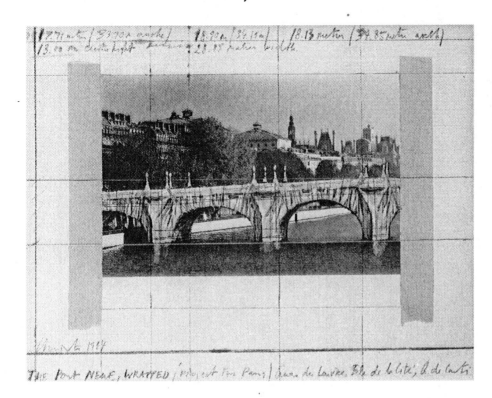

**Christo.
The Pont -Neuf
Wrapped, Project
for Paris, 1975–85.
Painted Photograph,
1984.**
This image exemplifies
another of Christo's
techniques for visualiz-
ing his projects in con-
text.

lotte Ellis, for example, wrote in the *RIBA Journal* that "there can be no doubt that Christo achieved his aim — getting people to rediscover the Pont Neuf."[23] Similarly, Michael Spens wrote in *Studio International* that the project, "was highly accessible. The crowds came, the traffic continued, there was popular acclaim — a rare double achievement. The 200,000 people per day who came to see the wrapping were in direct physical contact with the 'skin'."[24] And Jonathan Kuhn noted, "Central to his project is the shared physical and social

**Christo.
The Pont-Neuf
Wrapped, Project
for Paris, 1975–85.**
A view of the project
as installed. The
bridge was wrapped
in sandstone-colored
fabric.

**Christo.
The Pont-Neuf
Wrapped, Project
for Paris, 1975–85.**
A view of the project at
night.

effort, so that even the most passive participants (the onlookers) achieve the vicarious thrill of human potential."[25] But, he cautions, "We must not forget that the communal event began in the mind of one visionary artist."[26]

Christo was born in 1935 in Grabrovo, Bulgaria. He studied at the Fine Arts Academy in Sofia, before moving first to Prague, then to Vienna, where he studied at the Academy of Fine Arts for a semester, ending up in Paris in 1958. There he married Frenchwoman Jeanne-Claude de Guillebon, who became his business manager; the two settled permanently in New York City in 1964. The effect of his early experiences as an art student in Bulgaria can still be seen in Christo's wrappings and environmental art today. Addressing a particularly relevant experience that Christo had as a youth in the artist's brigades, Werner Spies writes:

While attending the Academy of Art in [1953–56] he regularly spent weekends with groups of students working in the country. Their job was to prettify the scenery along the route of the Orient Express through Bulgaria, to impress the travelers from capitalist countries. The students were sent to agricultural co-ops where they advised the farmers how to show off their tractors and other machinery to best advantage; they also showed them how to cover their haystacks with tarps in order to improve the rural landscape.[27]

Christo's early packaging in the service of socialism has now been transformed into a capitalist entrepreneurship on the grand scale in which he not only conceives and initiates projects, but takes charge of the financing and massive organizational effort required to bring them about.

Among the better known of Christo's large-scale environmental interventions is *Running Fence, Sonoma and Marin Counties, California, 1972–76,* an 18-foot high, 24.5-mile-long ribbon of fabric that crossed rolling hills on property belonging to fifty-nine different ranchers before dropping into the Pacific Ocean at Bodega Bay. The nature of Christo's art as action, not simply object, is reflected in the description of the *Running Fence* given in the project's press release:

The art project consisted of: forty-two months of collaborative efforts, the ranchers participation, eighteen Public Hearings, three sessions at the Superior Courts of California, the drafting of a four-hundred and fifty page Environmental Impact Report and the temporary use of the hills, the sky and the Ocean.[28]

Running Fence, like the *Pont-Neuf Wrapped,* was in place for fourteen days and when removed no evidence of the fence remained on the land.

Another of Christo's major environmental works was *Surrounded Islands, Biscayne Bay, Greater Miami, Florida, 1980–83.* Christo described the project in a press release: "On May 4, 1983, out of a total work force of 430, the unfurling crew began to blossom the pink fabric."[29] He further explained that eleven islands

have been surrounded with 6.5 million square feet of pink woven polypropylene fabric covering the surface of the water, floating and extending out 200 feet from each island into the Bay. The fabric has been sewn into 79 patterns to follow the contours of the 11 islands. For 2 weeks Surrounded Islands spreading over 7 miles is being seen, approached and enjoyed by the public, from the causeways, the land, the water and the air. The luminous pink color of the shiny fabric is in harmony with the tropical vegetation of the uninhabited verdant island, the light of the Miami sky and the colors of the shallow waters of Biscayne Bay.[30]

**Christo.
Running Fence,
Sonoma and Marin
Counties, California.
1972–1976.**
An aerial view of a
section of the 24.5-mile
long, 18-foot high ribbon
of white fabric.

101

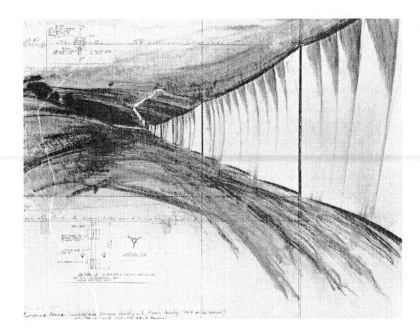

Recently completed was another major environmental project, this time on a global scale. *The Umbrellas, Joint Project for Japan and U.S.A.*, according to a press release issued before its completion, would consist of

3,100 octagonal umbrellas, 6 meters high (19 feet 8 inches) and 8.69 meters in diameter (28 feet 6 inches), [which] will meander in the landscape simultaneously, for about 19 kilometers (12 miles) in Japan and 29 kilometers (18 miles) in the U.S.A. The 1,340 blue umbrellas in Ibaraki and the 1,760 yellow umbrellas in California will be placed sometimes in clusters covering entire fields, or deployed in a line, or randomly spaced from each other, running alongside roads, villages, and river banks. . . . From October 8, 1991, for a period of three weeks, *The Umbrellas* will be seen, approached, and enjoyed by the

public, either by car from a distance and closer as they border the roads, or by walking under *The Umbrellas* in their luminous shadows.[31]

The estimated cost of the project was $26 million.

One of the most discussed, criticized, and misunderstood aspects of Christo's large-scale works is their financing. The fact that such large sums of money are devoted to temporary art installations very often provokes outraged responses. The fact that Christo himself spends all his money on his projects, and that the projects are erected only after years of patient consensus building with all parties to be affected by his work, seems to do little to assuage his critics. Responding to this criticism, Christo says:

People want to know why I don't give the money to the heart machine, or to society. First, I am not involved with the heart machine. I am involved with art. All artists need money to buy materials. My materials cost more. Also, people do not understand that when I propose the project, the money for it does not yet exist. It will be there only if I get permission, produce four hundred or five hundred drawings, and Jeanne-Claude sell them. Because I say in plain voice there is no way to make money from these projects, they are nervous and upset. If I say I spend three million and make a hundred million, like a movie producer, then this will be normal.[32]

In spite of the oft-voiced criticism of the cost of Christo's projects, once they have been realized most critics of Christo's work fall silent. As Werner Spies notes:

Christo and Jeanne-Claude Christo during the staking for "The Umbrellas, Joint Project for Japan and U.S.A." October 1988, Ibaraki, Japan.

The storms of protest that greeted Christo's earliest projects and that always gave way to wild enthusiasm are part of the mechanism of his success. The ritual and the procedure are by now familiar: wherever Christo appears and, with the help of a troop of assistants, undertakes his monumental interventions in people's accustomed lives, a bewildered and often furious uprising ensues. A pragmatic reckoning takes place. The culture of planned obsolescence demands permanence of art; Christo, out of a deep knowledge of his time, refuses to comply. Yet the initial fury soon subsides, making the work seem even more attractive and acceptable; from resistance and a lack of imaginative response the viewer moves to a feeling of sensual amazement. This process occurs time and again.[33]

The dual roles that Christo has taken on, that of fine artist *and* capitalist entrepreneur, are addressed by David Bourdon:

He is, to a certain extent, a traditional sculptor — working alone in his studio, making drawings, collages and scale models, the sale of which finances his projects. But once he has worked out on paper the concept for an extravaganza, and has raised the money, he is suddenly an entrepreneur — coordinating a team of engineers, building contractors, environmental consultants, lawyers and bureaucrats.[34]

Bourdon further notes that, "All of Christo's large projects are carefully planned in meticulously detailed studies, most often in the form of sketches, photomontages, relief-collages, and three-dimensional scale models."[35] Christo's graphic technique has evolved to suit the nature of his projects, serving both as a technique through which to communicate his intentions to his many collaborators and as a means of generating income to stage his projects. In his introduction to a book cataloging the prints and objects that are sold to finance Christo's work, Werner Spies describes the nature of Christo's smaller scale visual work:

The objects and prints are enormously diverse, as are the techniques and media employed. Yet rather than reflecting a concern for graphic innovation, this diversity arises directly from the process of planning, developing, and realizing the projects. The

activity of drawing and collage is a preparatory one with Christo. The designs he makes at this phase anticipate realization, representing imaginative projections of something that must first come to being. Yet they are not merely beautiful visions. On closer examination, we notice that these drawings, like architectural renderings or engineering sketches, contain much information about technical details. This sets them part from utopian designs. In preparing a project Christo makes sketches and pastes in the actual materials he plans to employ. He makes frequent use of topographic photographs, adding elements of drawing and collage, using the photograph as a background for his draftsmanship. . . .

Rapid, summary rendering ensures that the envisioned project will be stylistically adapted to its surroundings. The concern for the actual conditions of production, beyond the aesthetic effect of the result, gives rise to fascinating images that often, like encyclopedia illustrations, combine several sorts of information: an overall view, perspective renderings, and precise planning details.[36]

Despite the beauty and inventive nature of his visual work, Christo sees them as merely preliminary, and secondary, to the realization of his large-scale environmental interventions. He notes: "The drawings can never match the reality. It's so physical, so overwhelming — the power of the fabric, the cables, the site. It gives you a fantastic power of experience!"[37]

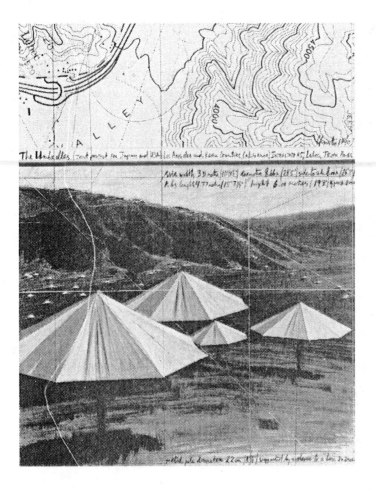

Christo.
The Umbrellas,
Joint Project for
Japan and U.S.A.
Collage in 2 Parts, 1990.
This collage depicts the
appearance and location
of some of the 1,760 yel-
low umbrellas to be
installed in California.

Even so, Christo prefers discussing the physical aspects of his work, listing square yards of fabric, feet of rope, numbers of workers, years of planning, and so on, to describing its purpose or meaning. Rarely does he discuss the reasons why he takes on such monumental yet ephemeral challenges. Addressing the *Running Fence* in an interview in *Domus*, however, Christo broached these issues perhaps as fully as he ever has:

Physically, Running Fence is a barrier 6 metres tall and 30 km long, in a landscape outside San Francisco, which crosses 14 roads, a small town, a highway and a State Road. But of course, Running Fence is not the poles, it's not the canvas or the cables; but the hills, the ocean, the land, the farms, the farmers, the roads, the landscape, the people and their relationships, I mean, there's an invisible part of Running Fence which is lived by a large part of the population, in the community where the project is rooted, where it is growing up. The project began with a simple idea. Almost all my projects are very simple, very easy to describe, excessively simple. . . . The project is truly lived by an enormous number of people who include our sixty farmers, hundreds of workers, the engineers, the lawyers, but also a whole group of people from the communities of Sonoma and Marin Counties who have been engaged in the project, in an almost subconscious dimension. You see, the project is rooted in the lives of these people. Generally the movements *for* or *against* actions like that occur when they want to build a new town or a new highway, that's to say, something that touches the population very rationally.

It's very exciting to see that happening with a project which is absolutely the height of irrationality . . . And to see a community of people engaged in an attitude for several months on end — in fact for almost three years now — when you think how very irrational the barrier really is. And all that great effort on the part of the government, to judge us, to investigate us to see if one is good or not good. . . . But all that is just art. There is not a single moment of "pragmatic use" for Running Fence, from start to finish. This isn't a wind-break or a barrier to keep the birds off or to serve some purpose other than art.

. . . The whole of this operation is a collective work, in the sense that this project has been carried out by a lot of people. If my sixty farmers had not agreed I would never have done this Running Fence. In all these months of dealings with these farmers, with our lawyers and our workers, with engineers, etc., an attitude has been built up to achieve the project's end. It's like an expedition, to reach the top of a mountain, to build up this enthusiasm, because the aim of the project is quite gratuitous. I think and I am absolutely sure that the project involves the subconscious of all these people who have never had any relations with art in a political state. They have the pleasure of following the battles with government, the oppositions, the successes and the difficulties, because the thought is always there in their minds: the barrier will be there one day. Besides, there is an irreplaceable thing: there is a dynamic dimension in their work: they are not spectators in front of the work of art, they are of *making* a work of art. All that means art, from start to finish.[38]

Christo emphasizes the processes, the human processes, involved in realizing his collaborative ventures as being the "art"; the physical artifact is a part, but only a transitory part, of the art experience. In other words, for those who experienced the project, *Running Fence* will live on long after the physical barrier, the art object, has been removed. This point is reinforced by Maudette Ball in her review of an exhibition featuring documentation of Christo's work. In an article titled "Documenting Evanescent Projects" she wrote of *Running Fence:*

Like most of Christo's works, it is as much about politics and social philosophy as about art. Christo and his partner Jeanne-Claude Christo, capitalists and entrepreneurs both, marshaled resources and made the system work for them with a tenacity that carried them through forty-two months of collaborative efforts. . . . Christo's projects, just like any large-scale public works such as bridges, are carefully organized and precisely executed. They differ substantially from government-run projects, however, because the spirit of the process is communal, the product evanescent. . . . The environment was borrowed, not irrevocably altered, but our perceptions of the environment were forever altered by the sinuous white line of *Running Fence* drawn across the dark land, changing and moving as it took color from a sunset or billowed like a wind-filled sail. The purpose of the work . . . was experiential, not functional.[39]

The nature of Christo's work is, perhaps, best summed up by Jonathan Fineberg:

Christo's work stands in contrast to the current enervated state of avant-gardism as a viable posture for making new art. With a Christo project, the directness of the experience, the feeling of participation, the visual beauty, all heighten the viewer's sense of being alive. Through the art work, he experiences the landscape, the politics, even people in a new and more profound way.[40]

Christo's work is particularly instructive for designers wishing to make the transition from an object orientation to a more contextual approach. As Lawrence Alloway noted in an early critique, "Gradually Christo moved away from the object."[41] A consequence of this transition is that "control passes from, say, the act of drawing to the act of contextualization."[42] Or, put more simply, "What Christo has done is to turn physical space into psychological response."[43] This is the essence of contextual design.

BRIAN ENO'S AMBIENT MUSIC, VIDEO, AND INSTALLATIONS

"Well it's very hard to know what to describe myself as," Brian Eno said. "I'm often faced with this problem in ordinary day-to-day situations. Like yesterday, I was coming from the station in a taxi and the guy said, 'Been anywhere nice?' and said, yeah, I've been out to the country. He said, 'Oh, do you live out there?' and I said, no, I have a studio there, but I live in London most of the time. And he said, 'Oh a studio, what do you do then?' and I said, well I'm an artist I guess and he says, 'Oh, painter?' I said no, not really a painter, and he said, 'Sculptor?' I said, no, not really a sculptor. I said, I use sound and light and of course then it got all very complicated and he said, 'Well what you do is like fireworks, is it?' Which actually was quite a good perception on his part."[44]

What Eno was struggling to describe simply was his recent work creating full-scale, multimedia installations intended to induce a sense of heightened perception in those who experience them. The main feature of the installations are "light sculptures," a hybrid media Eno created consisting of three-dimensional forms in a variety of shapes and sizes, either mounted on the wall or sitting on the floor. These forms are illuminated by gradually changing patterns and shades of light, most often from a television monitor concealed behind or below them. The visual effect of the light sculptures is of ever-evolving, luminous abstract paintings. The light sculptures are presented in darkened, cool spaces, that resonate with the quiet sound of Eno's ambient music. I visited one such installation, *Place #11*, at the Riverside Studios in London in 1986 and found the experience extremely pleasant and relaxing, but invigorating as well. I visited the installation several times and judging from their comments, both overheard and as recorded in the guest book Eno left at the gallery as a means of eliciting peoples' opinions, other visitors found the piece to be very engaging as well.

Eno has set up installations of this type in a number of cities in Europe, North America, and Japan, and the critical response to them has been overwhelmingly positive. Jacki Apple, for example, in reviewing Eno's installation *Latest Flames*, in Santa Monica, California, wrote that

Eno . . . is a conceptualist whose interest is in creating environments or 'settings' in which the audience has the opportunity to enter into a state of heightened sensual awareness and encounter the unfamiliar. Paradoxically his cool, pristine, formal aesthet-

**Portrait of Brian Eno
(London, 1987).**

ic produces meditational spaces that induce both an intensity of feeling and a harmonic sense of well-being. . . . Eno's work, which is at once esoteric and accessible seeks to unify experience and perception, body and mind, the analytic and the intuitive, the sensual and the spiritual. Thus minimalism and romanticism easily cohabit in the same piece. The audience is not a separate entity but an integral part of his conception, an active element. . . . The abstract images that seem to float in space are actually sculptural cardboard structures illuminated from underneath by video monitors that project changing hues of color. Each island of light is suspended in an all-pervasive cushion of ambient music, overlapping waves of sound that ebb and flow through the space. The hardware that produces all of this is nowhere in evidence. An overt display of technical virtuosity is antithetical to Eno's intentions. Technology is simply another tool in the service of the imagination. . . . *Latest Flames* does not pacify or tranquilize, offer vicarious living, or a means of escape. Instead it stimulates by directly sensitizing and intensifying one's perceptual awareness. It is about being in it, not watching it.[45]

Eno has on occasion described himself as a "synthesist," a term that well encompasses his broad background and diverse interests. Born in Woodbridge, Suffolk, England, he attended Ipswich Art School before taking his B.F.A. from Winchester School of Art in 1969. Soon, however, Eno was drawn away from painting to music. He described the transition:

By the mid-1960s, music was definitely the happening art. Painting seemed extremely cumbersome, bunged up with old ideas and incapable as a medium of responding to a new feeling that was moving through the arts. This new feeling was expressed by the motto "process not product." The movement represented a sense many people felt that the orientation towards producing objects was no longer exciting, and, instead, processes were becoming the interesting point of focus.[46]

Eno found in art school, as I did while studying architecture, great resistance to the transition from a product- to a process-oriented view:

Like the standard issue art teachers of the day, their interest was in seeing the object as the fruition of the artistic process. And because twentieth century art frequently does not observe this premise, they were floundering — trying to graft a redundant philosophy onto a set of events that it had not been designed for.[47]

109

Eno rejected the object orientation of the plastic arts and moved into music. After a two-year stint with the art rock group Roxy Music and a series of critically acclaimed solo pop albums, Eno chose to adopt a more contextual approach. One of the first of his albums of this type was *Discreet Music*, released in 1975. On this record he used a tape loop system of his own invention as the principal means of generating the music. On the album's cover notes he wrote:

Since I have always preferred making plans to executing them, I have gravitated towards situations and systems that, once set into operation, could create music with little or no intervention on my part. That is to say, I tend towards the roles of planner and programmer, and then become an audience to the results. . . . It is a point of discipline to accept this passive role, and, for once, ignore the tendency to play the artist by dabbling and interfering.[48]

Eno continued his experiments with more contextually oriented music by considering first the perceptual effects that he wished his music to have, then proceeding with the actual composition. In 1978 he released *Ambient 1: Music for Airports*, an album whose specific purpose was to inculcate certain specific perceptual experiences. Eno describes the concept of ambient music:

Over the past three years, I have become interested in the use of music as ambience, and have come to believe that it is possible to produce material that can be used thus without being in any way compromised. To create a distinction between my own experiments in this area and the products of the various purveyors of canned music, I have begun using the term Ambient Music. An ambience is defined as an atmosphere, or a surrounding influence: a tint. My intention is to produce original pieces ostensibly (but not exclusively) for particular times and situations with a view to building up a small but versatile catalogue of environmental music suited to a wide variety of moods and atmospheres.

Whereas the extant canned music companies proceed from the basis of regularizing environments by blanketing their acoustic and atmospheric idiosyncrasies, Ambient Music is intended to enhance these. Whereas conventional background music is produced by stripping away all sense of doubt and uncertainty (and thus all genuine interest) from the music, Ambient Music retains these qualities. And whereas their intention is to "brighten" the environment by adding stimulus to it (thus supposedly alleviating the tedium of routine tasks and levelling out the natural ups and downs of the body rhythms) Ambient Music is intended to induce calm and a space to think. Ambient

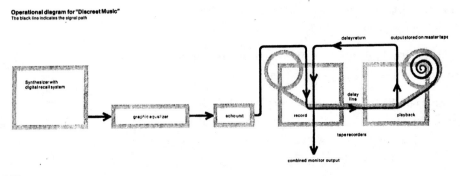

Operational diagram for "Discreet Music"
The black line indicates the signal path

Brian Eno. Operational Diagram for "Discreet Music." This diagram, which illustrates the system used to produce the *Discreet Music* album, reflects Eno's interest in compositional processes.

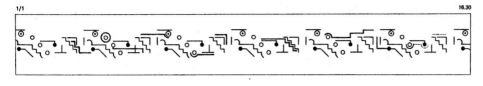

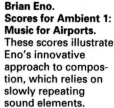

Brian Eno.
Scores for Ambient 1:
Music for Airports.
These scores illustrate Eno's innovative approach to composition, which relies on slowly repeating sound elements.

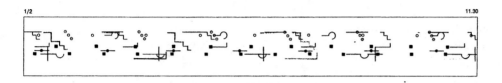

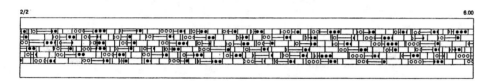

Music must be able to accommodate many levels of listening attention without enforcing one in particular; it must be as ignorable as it is interesting.[49]

To date Eno has released four albums in the Ambient Music series, each of which caters to different moods. To supplement his experiments with ambient music, Eno developed nonnarrative video pieces that have been installed in a variety of settings, including airports, hospitals, and museums. The videos are presented on a television monitor in a vertical orientation. I saw one of these early video pieces, *Mistaken Memories of Mediaeval Manhattan,* at the Stedelijk Museum in Amsterdam in 1982 and found it a very unusual but engaging experience. The image consisted of a view of the Manhattan skyline from an apartment window taken by a single video camera that did not move. On the monitor an image of a skyscraper was present, clouds entered and left the picture, and the tone on the image seemed to change gradually, but there was no "action," or a story as such. Eno's ambient-style music played throughout the video showing.

In a recent interview Eno explained his reasons for developing videos to accompany his ambient music:

That was quite an easy transition, as a matter of fact, because one of the keynotes of the idea of ambient music is the notion of creating an environmental music, a music which is all around you and lasts for a very long time. It's a kind of music that you walk into and it's deliberately meant to have that kind of effect of being like a gas of some kind, you walk into the gas. So it wasn't at all a stretch of the imagination to think of making that in three dimensions. I experimented with that, oh quite a few years ago now, working with more than a simple stereo-speaker system, having several different sound sources and positioning them in all sorts of places so you kind of walk through the music. The act of listening became an active journey through a piece of music, that was the idea. The beginning of working with video was actually from noticing that a camera looking out of a window and not doing anything televisual like panning or zooming or editing or all the other things which one associates with camera practice normally was actually very engaging. I actually liked looking at the screen there and just sitting and watching nothing much going on. It turned landscape into painting in a way that I enjoyed. I started doing installations at the end of the seventies with the results of the tapes that I had made, with actually just having my camera pretty much just sitting in the window sill. What I liked about those pieces was that they gave you a different feeling about television. They moved television away from being a narrative medium to being a pictorial one. Now this is very similar to what I think was happening with ambient music where you gave up the idea of music being a sort of structured narrative through a plot with climaxes and surprises and new things coming in and going out and a big ending of some kind. You gave up that idea and instead you said, here is a condition of some kind, here is an ambience, stick it on and you can enter into it if you choose or you can look away from it if you choose. The first videos I did were static shots of rooftops in Manhattan, and the idea with those things is that they functioned very much as a kind of window. It was something that curiously enough hadn't been tried with video before, the idea of just leaving the camera alone and letting the picture develop in its own way.[50]

I then asked how the videos evolved into the full-scale installations and Eno stated:

That came about because though I was very pleased with the feeling of these video paintings I was making, I also was interested in the idea that one might do the same thing without using images. Now, this came about from a specific problem I had to solve. I was asked to do an exhibition of those video works with a friend of mine who's a painter. So the idea was that he would show his paintings and I would show some of those video pictures. The problem was that television really requires or enforces a different way of looking than paintings do. You look *at* a painting but you look *into* a television screen and they just didn't look good together to me, it was a very unhappy mixture. One of the reasons it was unhappy is that the TV monitor is so overpowering because it's radiant light, it's not reflected light, it's radiant light and it kind of sucks all the attention in a room towards itself. I thought this just made the paintings look dead, which was very far from what they were, they were very lively paintings, but next to a television screen they didn't work. So I started to try to think of a way of using the TV in a way that was not based on images, was not based on pictures of other things, and so that's when I started making constructions on the television screen that were internally lit by the screens themselves, so I used the TV as a light source. What's good about that idea is that the TV is actually the most controllable light source we have. If you ask a lighting engineer how difficult it is to control lights very exactly you realize it's a very complicated technology. But television, of course, is a way of controlling light very, very, very precisely so I kind of lucked into a very powerful technology there, it had never been used for exactly what I was doing before, but it has a lot of power in that direction.[51]

When asked to envisage possible future developments of the ambient concept, Eno responded:

Well I think one of the things that I'm thinking about a lot at the moment is the idea of hypertext. Hypertext as a concept interests me a lot because I'm fascinated in thinking about whether that can be applied to music, the idea of presenting a music that is rather than a "piece," a composed piece, is a set of acoustic possibilities that you can work your way through. The way you can imagine it in a physical sense is if there were a huge room and in the ceiling and the floor were thousands of loudspeakers, so there would be one in the ceiling and its companion, its stereo pair as it were in the floor. So each one of those speakers, or each pair of those speakers, has a unique source and so by moving around in the space, you choose the piece of music that you move through. This is technically fairly involved at the moment, but I see that kind of future as very exciting, the idea of creating "sculptural music," if you like — active music.[52]

I asked Eno if this idea was a development of the music system used in his installations, such as *Place #11*, in which unsynchronized cassettes of ambient-style music played in each of the four corners of the space, causing the music "mix" to vary depending upon where one is in the space. He replied:

That's right. And in fact a lot of my installations have used that idea, but there's a limit to how large the spaces are, you don't ever get separation — I mean it works fine, but you don't get radical differences from one side of the room to another. I would really like the idea of a situation in which you really could move through a piece of music and end up in quite a different musical place from where you started. The only time I've done anything like that especially was in Rome. I had an installation at the Orto Botanico, which is a big botanical garden, and I had two completely different pieces of music playing there and in the center I had a third piece which actually mediated between them, so though those two pieces were quite incompatible, I made this piece that sat in the middle out of the few common elements between them. So at the bottom you would hear piece "A," in the middle you would hear this hybrid, and then you could walk out of there and you would finally be in piece "B" without noticing that you actually gone through a complete sort of modal shift of some kind. The only reason that could work was because it was a very big space and it was outdoors so one wasn't dealing with acoustic reflection at all.[53]

Another possible future development of the ambient concept that Eno has proposed are "quiet clubs," which would be similar to his installations but permanent. Eno described the purpose of these clubs to Rick Poynor:

I keep thinking about discotheques. They have the wrong ambience but they are the right kind of place. Imagine if there were clubs you could go to which were as designed as discos and as carefully thought-out in terms of decor and stimulus, presentation and music — that had that level of attention — but did other things. So the result they produced in you was different.[54]

A few possible locations for such clubs are under discussion, but there are as yet no firm plans to build one.

In all of Eno's work, regardless of media, his main interest is in bringing about certain perceptual effects in those who experience them. In fact, the evolution of his work, and his choice of media, has been predicated on the type of effect he has sought to inculcate. As indicated in his description of the compositional process for *Discreet Music,* Eno is very explicit about the processes of composition used in his work. Similarly, as borne out in his comments about the purpose of ambient music, he is equally concerned with the perceptual effects his music has. I questioned him about the nature of the connection between the processes of composition used in his work and the process of perception he seeks to bring about through his work. He responded:

Well, I think it's intuitive in the sense that it's always being mediated by my feelings about the results of the processes. I'm always thinking up processes but what's also important is what inputs go into those processes. If you think of that way of writing music as a kind of machine, one is building machines, but these machines are transforming machines, you put certain information in one end and it comes out patterned and configured in certain ways at the other end. I think what happened with a lot of minimal, process, and systems composers is that they were extremely interested in the type of machine and very uninterested in the input, in fact to the point where it was considered rather a dereliction of duty to even think about what the input was. The position was that you must concentrate on the system, on the process, then anything can go into it. John Cage is an example of somebody who thought that way to an extent, but a lot of other composers did as well. It struck me quite a long time ago that if you did that the listenability of the results was entirely dependent on whether you happened by chance to choose inputs that had some intrinsic interest. I'm sure you've seen the type of things where people have very, very complex machines that respond to your movement in a room and to the temperature and to whether you're wearing a red tie or not, these kind of very sophisticated electronic music machines and in the end what you get out of them is "beep," "errn," "pllp," "doonk," "grrk," "sch," "nnt" and I think, so what? Whenever I got the "so what?" feeling I thought there's something not right here; if after all that you think "so what?" it's not working. It's not enough just to make a clever machine, I want to make music that keeps me coming back to it and keeps me excited about it. So I spend a lot of time thinking about what goes into the machine as well. You know, what drives it.[55]

When asked how — by what process — he judges the listenability of his music, or the success of the ambiences he creates, Eno said:

That's based on what happens to me when I'm looking at or listening to the work. I usually think, well if this is what happens to me then probably something like that will happen to other people as well. But a lot of things condition the way I work: Where is it going? What is it for actually? What is it meant to do in the world? How am I hoping other will deal with it or receive it? What do I want to happen to them?[56]

I asked Eno if he had an overriding term for his ambient work, music, videos, and installations, and he responded:

I don't really, no. One of the reasons for that is because it changes shape quite a lot. The last couple of installations I did — one was in Montreal, the other was in Tokyo — had actually quite a different mood to them and they weren't at all as pastoral, or as relaxing I would say, as other ambient stuff I've done. They were much more — sharp, not aggressive exactly, but unsettling, I would say. I think this is a mood that I wouldn't have seen as part of the ambient thing a few years ago. I have to be a bit careful about describing it too closely because I don't want to hem myself in.[57]

Presently Eno divides his time between producing installations, making music, writing, and consulting work:

One of the problems with installations is that whether I do them or not depends on whether I get invited to or not. Because they always depend on using some kind of a public space, those kinds of things are usually mapped out fairly far in advance, a year in advance or something like that. So what I do now is I just say, from September to May I'll do installations, the rest of the time I'll do music. What was happening with the installations is that they'd be dotted throughout the year and it meant that I never got a consistent period to think about music again.[58]

Eno's recent musical efforts have included producing albums for the group U2, as well as a return to making pop records himself, including *Wrong Way Up*, a collaboration with John Cale that was released in 1990.

Eno has described himself as "someone who enjoys putting things together, just taking things from different places and seeing what happens when you put them together."[59] This broad scope is reflected in some of Eno's recent writings, yet to be published, whose topics include hypertext, pornography, prohibition, the Gulf War, and the social, cultural, and perceptual effects of music, painting, and literature. Another current project, which he is working on with Peter Gabriel, is a "theme park for the arts" to be constructed in Barcelona. Eno also recently participated in a conference held by Nissan. Commenting on this he said:

The Nissan thing came about because I belong to this network called GBN, Global Business Network, which is a think tank which advises various kinds of businesses on what sort of futures there might be. Nissan had commissioned the think tank to talk about the future of car design, or the future of transport in general actually, which is what it became soon enough. So I was chosen to be one of the contributors to that.[60]

I remarked that I found it very encouraging that someone would be selected on the basis of their intelligence and creativity, rather than simply because they possessed certain professional qualifications. Eno concurred: "It's great, isn't it? I can't tell you how encouraging I find it because I don't have any professional background!"[61]

Through his development of ambient music, videos, and full-scale, multimedia installations Brian Eno has sought to provide contexts for progressively heightened perceptual experience. His ability to change aims and methods freely in order to realize the perceptual effects he desires has been central to the success of Eno's work. This ability is also a necessary precursor to any successful contextual design.

FROM FORM TO EXPERIENCE

There is much to be enjoyed in, and learned from, the work of Robert Wilson, Christo, and Brian Eno. All share an interest in inculcating perceptual experience through their work, and all of it is collaborative in nature, though in a much broader and more profound sense than has been realized in environmental design. As an indication of the direction in which a more contextually oriented design might develop, however, a few aspects of their work are especially important.

Wilson, in rejecting architecture, has opted in his theater pieces to design in space *and* time, setting up contexts in which each person viewing his works is effectively a collaborator, creating their own equally valid meaning or interpretation of it. Similarly Christo, in his large-scale projects, engages whole communities in the production of his grand collaborative efforts. Though the temporary realization of his ephemeral interventions is critical, the processes of their creation and perception are equally important. Brian Eno also adopted a contextual approach with his development of ambient music, video, and installations as contexts through which to induce "calm and a space to think." Eno's work is especially interesting for the way he has tailored his means and methods to realize his perceptual aims.

What these artists' work has in common is an abandonment of the object or product as the principal outcome of the creative process. An art "work" may exist, but only as a catalyst to perceptual experiences. This point is illustrated by a story Jeanne-Claude Christo told me. At one time NASA asked Christo if he would like to do a project on the moon. He rejected this suggestion for two reasons. First, he does not accept commissions of any kind for his work, but, second, and more importantly in this context, he rejected the idea because there were no people on the moon to experience the project, therefore there was no reason to do it. As with the work of Wilson and Eno, Christo's work is predicated on an *interaction* between people and contexts — designing the means of interaction is the artist's role, the interaction itself is their purpose.

In forming his view of what contextual designing could be, John Chris Jones has been greatly influenced by the concepts and approaches of number of contemporary artists. Commenting on his adoption of one technique used by many avant-garde artists, the use of chance in composition, Jones writes:

What's nice about it is that zen sense of concrete surprise at what emerges if one decides to trust not one's preconceptions but the situation itself. Using one's judgement to devise not the product but the learning process. Context designing, as I've recently begun to call it. A giving up of self-expression, ego, etc. by users as well as by professionals. Expecting what one discovers to change oneself as well as the situation. Removing from the scene the BLOCK, the limiting self-image, the only real obstacle, and letting oneself become, becoming more, the self becoming public, mythical, a part of all that is, a part that flows, does not obstruct.[62]

When I asked Jones to sum of the essence of this approach he said, "To my mind contextual design is reading the situation, making yourself a vehicle so that the situation designs itself, and the human mental obstacles are being undone and unravelled."[63]

Though contextual approaches to design are still somewhat underdeveloped, the concept of the design of experience, which Jones terms "intangible design," has begun to be addressed, especially in relation to newly emerging tasks, such as the design of computer software. While by no means well established, some approaches that focus on the design of user experience over time have been developed and will be reviewed in the following chapter.

6. Intangible Design

DEFINING INTANGIBLE DESIGN

Intangible design is the design of experience itself. Whereas most collaborative design efforts are focused on the built environment and contextual designs are aimed at heightening perceptual experience, intangible designs are, as John Chris Jones puts it, "designs-in-space-and-time,"[1] the "invisible" designs that complement a process, such as the use of a piece of computer software. Jones further notes that intangible design is concerned with "the scale of the system, the scale of the invisible and intangible patterns of experience and use."[2] Objects or products may be present in an intangible design, but as with the physical aspects of a contextual design, they are always of secondary importance to the experience of the system as a whole, over time. Through intangible design, peoples' experiences and actions, rather than technological capability or geometrical criteria, become the basis for designing.

The essence and importance of the intangible was well expressed by Lao Tzu in his book *Tao Teh Ching,* written in the sixth century B.C.

> Thirty spokes converge upon a single hub;
> It is on the hole in the center that the use of
>   the cart hinges.
>
> We make a vessel from a lump of clay;
> It is the empty space within the vessel that makes it
>   useful.
>
> We make doors and windows for a room;
> But it is the empty spaces that make the room livable.
>
> Thus, while the tangible has advantages,
> It is the intangible that makes it useful.[3]

Unlike design approaches that principally address the tangible aspects of designing — physical and material features such as spokes and hubs, clay, or doors and windows — the focus of intangible designing is on use, and usefulness.

The notion of intangible design has broad applicability. As noted earlier, traditional design approaches focus on the production of form; there is nothing in their methods that explicitly addresses use. When the nature of design tasks changes from the shaping of objects to the dynamic function of a system over time, object oriented design methods prove to be completely inapplicable. A range of alternative approaches have emerged independently in response to these new requirements for design. Among these are: user centered system design, humanware, and transparency.

User centered system design is a term suggested by Donald Norman and Stephen Draper, both of them cognitive scientists. They write in introducing their eponymously titled anthology:

This is a book about the design of computers, but from the user's point of view. . . . The emphasis is on people, rather than technology, although the powers and limits of contemporary machines are considered in order to know how to take that next step from today's limited machines toward more user-centered ones. . . . We wish to attempt User Centered System Design, to ask what the goals and needs of the users are, what tools they need, what kind of tasks they wish to perform, and what methods they would prefer to use. We would like to start with the users, and to work from there.[4]

Addressing the topic of human-computer interaction, they write:

People are quite different from computers. This is hardly a novel observation, but whenever people use computers, there is necessarily a zone of mutual accommodation and this defines our area of interest. People are so adaptable that they are capable of shouldering the entire burden of accommodation to an artifact, but skillful designers make large parts of this burden vanish by adapting the artifact to its users. To understand successful design requires an understanding of the technology, the person, and their mutual interaction.[5]

Norman and Draper are exploring this mutual interaction from an academic perspective but, thus far, their ideas have been realized only to a limited extent in practice.

In Japan a design philosophy termed "humanware" has emerged that shares many of the goals of user centered system design and that *has* been fully embraced by industry. Kiyoshi Sakashita, for example, Director of Sharp's industrial design think tank, writes:

Sharp's designers are moving from a hardware role to a software role — what we call humanware. The idea of humanware is an appeal to the aesthetic sense, emotions, the cultural values of human beings. By considering the human feeling and mentality we aim to promote the development of merchandise that can really satisfy people's needs.[6]

Another Japanese company pursuing this approach is Mazda, which is explicitly focusing on the quality of experience their cars provide and using this as a basis for design. An article in *The Economist* reported:

Mazda is the biggest exponent of *kansei,* which it says is best interpreted as "sensitivity". Like other carmakers, Mazda fits out its test cars with sensors to detect quantifiable things, such as vibration levels, which are transmitted by radio links to a data-processing centre as cars meet various driving conditions, from mountainous roads to motorways.

But as Mazda's cars go around the test track their drivers also give a running commentary into a microphone to provide subjective reactions. . . .

Physical and emotional responses to different colours, shapes and even the smells inside a car are now being measured. Cameras have been used to follow the eye movements of people looking at new designs. Synthesizers have been used to reproduce various sounds in order to try and determine the most desirable engine noise for people of different ages and backgrounds.[7]

The extent to which a perceptual and experiential approach to designing at Mazda takes precedence over the planning of "dream" or "concept" cars on a drawing board is further borne out by Sheridan Tatsuno in his book *Created in Japan:* "'High-Sense' . . . is becoming a new consumer ethic. Mazda, for example, is a pioneer in the emerging field of 'sensory' engineering: the development of new products that appeal to the five human senses."[8] In summing up Japan's aims for its humanware philosophy, and its projected impact on the global market, Tatsuno asserts:

The biggest challenge from Japan will not be technical, but psychological and social. Just as the computer industry is shifting its focus from hardware to software and "groupware," we will see the rise of a Japanese "humanware" industry — the creation of new products and services that contribute to greater social and physical well-being. . . . Humanware engineering could well become a major growth industry in the twenty-first century, on the scale of the Industrial Revolution. A global creativity revolution would be its precursor.[9]

As reflected in these comments, the humanware philosophy is extremely broad in scope and intent and, if realized, could have profound implications, not only for design but also for life as a whole.

At the present time, however, perhaps the most fully realized of the new approaches to design of intangibles is transparency. This term is used by John Rheinfrank of Fitch RichardsonSmith's Exploratory Design Lab (EDL) to describe his group's work. The work of the EDL, and the principles behind it, will be explored in detail in the following section.

TRANSPARENCY

In transparent design the intangible processes of use explicitly guide the development of tangible artifacts. Though not widely discussed or as yet considered part of the mainstream, transparency in design is being pursued by a few firms. One of the most innovative of such firms is Fitch RichardsonSmith's Exploratory Design Lab, based in Worthington, Ohio. EDL does advanced product development for a number of major high-technology firms, including Apple Computer, Eastman Kodak, IBM, Philips, and Xerox. It should be emphasized that EDL's role is *not* to design the technology upon which the products depend, nor is it simply to do a traditional job of industrial-design styling of the exterior of machines. Rather, they *re-register product classes*, beginning with the social embedding and processes of use, then evolve new types of technologies to support them. The broad scope of EDL's work is reflected by the diversity of the educational backgrounds represented in their "design" team. These include: psychology, anthropology, urban design, graphic design, systems engineering, industrial design, linguistics, computer science, product design, architecture, and media science.

One of the keys to EDL's work, which leads to the realization of transparency, is the co-production or co-development of projects with representatives of the client firm and with potential users of the technology being evolved. This process is really a special, elaborate case of collaborative designing. John Rheinfrank, a co-founder of EDL and an executive vice president with Fitch RichardsonSmith, in discussing how his group goes about coproducing or codeveloping their work, said:

That's probably the most important form of work we do. To involve the client, we set up a project space that is used as an arena for the envisionment and embodiment of proto-types. We work very hard to get the client's internal developers engaged with this new content that we are developing. If we are working with a consumer products company and we are trying to re-register an entire class of consumer products, such as consumer electronics, what we do is, in a very honest way, draw the internal developers into the re-registration process. We have workshops with them, content and assumption chal-lenging workshops. We are doing much more than presenting to them, asking them to be passive learners. They're active learners — they're actually pulling in content and they're shifting the schema or framework that we're using, introducing the discontinuity that we're all after.

The other domain of co-development is the one where "customers," qua "users," qua "people with need" are involved, are brought into the development process. We're look-ing at some really radical changes in the notion of what market research is. What we're doing is involving potential users/customers in workshop formats very early and very late and all the times in between. We have them contribute to the shaping of the ideas. We conduct ethnographic studies where they're idealizing about the future at the same time we're observing very carefully what they're doing today. . . .

One of the things that we can do in our workshops with customers and users and internal developers is embody their tacit knowledge, building things we call "designs." Essentially what we're doing is grinding a set of eyeglasses together, finding a way of seeing the world, developing a set of assumptions and underlying rules. We call this a design language. You can call it what you want to, but you always have to call it some-thing. In a project that we're doing now with a consumer products company we're call-ing it a "platform for innovation."[10]

An example of a co-developed project was "Learning and Technology: new perspectives" for Apple Computer, which was voted Best of Category for Research in *ID* magazine's 1991 Annual Design Review. EDL involved a six-teen-year-old student and an experienced teacher in the project's development from the outset. Rheinfrank described the process that was followed:

We were inventing a technology that would become embedded within an idealized learning environment. So, it's essentially designing from an idealization of how learning

**Exploratory Design Lab.
Presentation from
"Learning and
Technology: new
perspectives" project
for Apple Computer.**
This prototype was cre-
ated by EDL to commu-
nicate their project
findings to the "internal
developers" at Apple
Computer.

happens — our best understanding of how learning actually happens, and how people's learning capacities are best developed. We did this instead of taking an existing technology, call it a computer, and looking at how to modify that technology so that it's most useful in learning environments. We exactly reversed the traditional "technology for its own sake" approach to doing development and came out with a quite surprising target for Apple to move towards.[11]

I asked Rheinfrank for a definition of the term "transparency" in relation to the work of EDL. He replied:

There are three areas in which I think transparency exists — I can give you a kind of ontology of transparency as I'm beginning to understand it. I really see transparency as a very much emerging concept in the design of what I term "new technical objects." In our use of a machine like a computer, there should be a kind of a *subject matter transparency*. There's a chance that you could have a great deal of technical and other types of detail made available to you in ways that associate it with the subject matter that you are dealing with. So when you are using this machine you can see through several layers of internal detail, however deep or shallow you want to go. You can essentially work your way around a subject matter space and bring pieces of it forward, using them to support your activity and the goals you're trying to achieve.[12]

One project in which EDL focused on subject matter transparency involved the development of a user interface for ECHO, an Electronic Claims Handling Office. The interface being designed was for an electronic claims-handling environment to be used by insurance companies. In designing this interface, EDL first developed an understanding of the activities involved in claims handling. Then, specific interface elements were created to support those activities. Thus, the interface contained representations of familiar objects such as files, file fold-

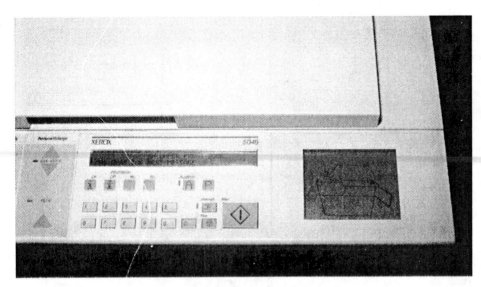

Exploratory Design Lab. Interactive windows on Xerox 5046 photocopier.
The window on the right features an animated diagram that, along with the text window on the top, gives interactive instructions the machine's operations.

ers, reports, and log books, and these objects were given new behaviors and capabilities to support claims handling and supervisory activities. In addition, a new visual element, called a milestone, was created, which indicated that a certain point in a claims-handling procedure had been reached. These milestones could be used to divide a claim into manageable chunks, and each claim could be quickly reviewed just in terms of the milestones that had been reached in handling the claim. Furthermore, the milestones themselves provided a way of structuring the claims handling procedure, so that organizations could identify what milestones they wanted to use and how they would be organized. The elements in the ECHO interface thus reflected the subject matter of case handling, helping claims handlers better understand and manage their work.

Rheinfrank continued his definition of transparency:

The next item would be the transparency of the technology itself: *technical transparency*. If I'm using a word processing program or some kind of algorithm to analyze data, that technology should also be transparent. I can get deep into the underlying models that produce it and make changes them, say using some kind of object oriented language, to wrap it around myself in a special way. It is a kind of a radically customized technical solution that is quite possible with all the computing power that we have available to us today. So it's a skillful blending of understanding and doing at the level of the production of a technology. You probably can't do that with a TV set attached to a typewriter keyboard, which is basically the prevailing metaphor available for users of computers.[13]

In the design of a series of copier-interface design concepts for Xerox, for example, EDL built an interactive "window" through which the user could learn about the technology without consulting a manual. The user is informed "through the window" of the status of the machine's operation — what size paper and how many copies have been selected, and how to orient the paper on the glass — and also has the option of getting more information. The user is notified "through the window" when the machine is out of paper and into which drawer replacement paper should be placed. Similarly, and most helpfully, in the event of a paper jam the user is shown, through an animated diagram, where in the machine the jam is and is given step-by-step instructions on how to remove the obstruction. This design with its interactive "window" demonstrates the way in which technical transparency can be used to support the development of new understandings.

Rheinfrank developed this concept of technical transparency more fully in an unpublished manuscript titled "Situated Languages for the Design of Computer-Human Interfaces," which he coauthored with Katherine Welker and Stuart Card. They wrote:

[Situated] Interface design languages . . . may provide an opportunity for users to play a role in the design process. With an interface design language, the technology is available for users to design the elements in the interface or the rules for interacting with them. If they add elements to the interface that have never been present within it, or if they change the rules for interaction in novel ways, they will actually be changing not just the interface itself, but also the design language used to generate the interface.[14]

Or, put more simply:

Situated languages . . . result in the creation of user interfaces in which design and implementation are tightly intertwined at every step. If coproduced by users and designers, these languages enable users to be active players in the design of the interfaces and objects with which they interact.[15]

Rheinfrank concludes his ontology of transparency by saying:

The next area which I think is probably the least understood and probably the most critical is *social transparency:* the social structure, the social web, within which the technology is embedded. What would we have as a technology if it revealed the web of understanding within which it evolves? Again, I'll use the term "technical object," say it's an answering machine or a word processor or telephone or whatever. You could essentially go out on that web and participate in a kind of forum in which you could increase your capacity to understand and use that technology. We're very much intrigued with the idea of harnessing the tacit knowledge which occurs naturally in the culture in the form of new technical objects that rapidly acquire cultural prominence. We're trying to accelerate their occurrence, to have them occur in a much more intelligent way, and we're trying to make those frameworks for the work of these companies we call our clients.

What makes a technology particularly powerful and self defining? Fax machines, for example, have had to take on a life of their own actually to participate in the production of more tacit knowledge. Answering machines are another example — they have quickly become established not just as devices for taking messages (as they were originally conceived) but also as devices for screening calls. It seems like the kinds of objects that have social transparency are the ones which really catch on in a work culture, a family setting, or whatever; things that have in their own existence the capacity to be something else. But that something else is radically under-determined, rather than over-determined. That seems to be another aspect of transparency.[16]

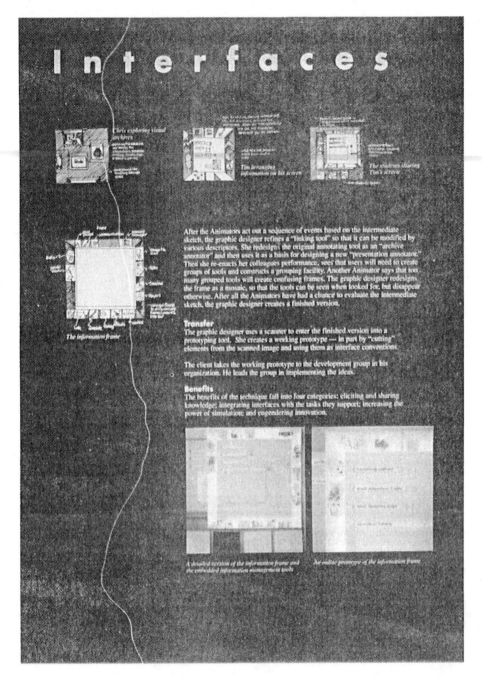

Exploratory Design Lab. "Animating Interfaces" project presentation. In this project, EDL set out principles for the design of an animated interface.

Much of the intellectual stimulus for these transparency concepts has come from Rheinfrank's association with the Institute for Research on Learning, and in particular Etienne Wenger and John Seeley Brown.

Because of the highly situated nature of the design tasks EDL undertakes it is very difficult to generalize from one project to another. Reporting on the firm's work is further complicated because many of their ongoing projects are confidential. Two key aspects that seem to be common to all of EDL's work, however, are their use of design languages and of physical prototypes. Not surprisingly, John Rheinfrank cites Christopher Alexander's pattern language, with its explicit linkage of patterns of events to patterns of space, as an influence on the group's work. In fact EDL collaborated with Alexander's Center for Environmental Structure on a "Future Workplace" project for furniture manufacturer Haworth.

More surprisingly, perhaps, EDL always construct physical prototypes that embody their design ideas in order to begin a dialogue of response from people. In discussing this I commented to Rheinfrank: "It seems that all of your projects are conceptual, but they are not abstract. To me that's the big surprise. The net result of that is there is no applicability gap, as present in much early design research which was done in the abstract and never applied. It seems you never do anything in the abstract even though it's all highly conceptual."[9] He responded, "That's right, it is highly conceptual. It's about re-registration, but at the end of the day it's very concrete. There may be abstractions used as explanations and as kinds of tools, but they are very quickly replaced by models or by sketches or running prototypes."[17]

I further observed: "I suppose another thing that I'm surprised about is that these complex processes, and the social understanding behind them, can be so readily embodied in objects. I would have thought that the object would have left out some of these things, but I guess that's the key to what you're doing, to make sure that they are built in." To which he replied, "Yes, and it actually is one of the most difficult parts of what we're doing, to make sure that they are present, essentially that the representations embody the conceptualizations."[18]

EDL's work with transparency provides a concrete example of how designing can be turned inside out, through the tailoring of the tangible aspects of designing — form, materials, and technology — to the intangible processes of experience and use. The implications of this transition for design are profound. As Rheinfrank and his co-authors write, "These new understandings are leading to a re-registration of attention to user-centered as activity-oriented design — design that enables people to work, play, learn and engage in other activities as fully as they possibly can."[19]

SOFTECNICA

As John Rheinfrank noted of his work on transparency in design, the newly emerging information technologies provide an opportunity, should we choose to act on it, to change the relationship between people and machines radically. With the advent of firms such as EDL, it seems that the nature of technology, and in consequence the nature of designing, may finally be changing, becoming more responsive to the dynamic processes of user experience. John Chris Jones has addressed this theme since his earliest writings in the 1950s, theorizing about ways of softening the impact of technology, making it more responsive to people instead of, as has largely been the case, forcing people to adapt to the requirements of technology.

Jones uses the term *softecnica* to describe a condition in which technology explicitly supports user activities:

. . . book, clock, phone, tv, computer, credit card, game, pill, and process. The soft technologies, or some of them. Not that the names of the products, the objects, gives the feel of them. That is more evident in the verbs, the processes: printing, publishing, reading, "what time is it?", phoning, watching TV, computing, programming, credit-rating, cash-dispensing, playing space invaders, taking the pill, designing the process. What is it that these have in common? Most obviously, I'd say, it is that they are non-mechanical, not depending on wheels, gears, pistons, rivets, or heat engines, but on electric power, on currents, complex circuits, minute components, invisible processes, relativities (in place of absolute standards), and on finding external analogues and processes fast and delicate enough to be matched to the operations of the eye, the ear, the brain, or any other organ of the body.[20]

The contrast between the nature of the newly emerging soft technologies such as computers and their industrial predecessors was also addressed by J. David Bolter in his book *Turing's Man: Western Culture in the Computer Age:*

Unlike the . . . steam engine, the computer is not a fixed mechanism. The genius of the von Neumann machine is that the program (operating instructions) and the data are stored in the same binary code and loaded together into the memory, and this coding means that the program can be altered as easily as the data, indeed, that there is no logical difference between the two. . . . The computer can be changed simply by loading a new program, and each new program makes the computer into a new machine. A programmer is a designer who has the remarkable advantage of being able to test his design as soon as it is specified. For the design *is* the program, written in a suitable language such as PASCAL, and he need only submit the program to the computer to find his machine realized. Furthermore, since a program itself is simply a series of binary digits, the computer can be programmed to write its own programs. The equivalent process in a steam engine would be to throw the gears into the furnace along with the coal and to expect the engine to produce by itself a design for a new machine.[21]

To bring about this radical change in the nature of technology requires a new sensitivity that was lacking in the industrial era. Jones, for example, writes:

Software. The word, like others coming from computing and the new technologies, implies a far more than accidental change from the rigid to the gentle, the mechanical to the automatic, the imposed to the adaptive. But can we rise to it? Are we, by our inheritance and experience of the harsher technologies of coal, and steam, and iron, by our acceptance of specialization as norm, so far adapted to all those things and practices that we have lost the original basis of organic adaptiveness that enabled us to put up with them? Is it possible to undo all that, to recover mind, and the freely adaptive body of the child, the pre-industrial, in reacting to the so unexpected flexibilities that now appear?[22]

Bolter also addressed this point, noting, "Paradoxically, there are aspects of electronic technology leading us away from the thinking of the recent past and closer to the ancient world."[23] He further writes, "Here again, technology and philosophy interact. The computer, the most philosophical of machines with its preoccupations with logic, time, space, and language, suggests a new view of human craftsmanship and creativity as well."[24]

This paradoxical return to craft, which the new technologies necessitate, echoes the desire of the early design methodologists to recover the trial-and-error spirit of craftwork. The extent to which this has in fact been realized is addressed by Jones:

The more I see of software designing the more I notice resemblance not to design in other fields but to craftsmanship. In each the designing, if such it can be called, is done by the maker, and there is much fitting, adjusting, adapting of existing designs, and much collaboration, with little chance of a bird's eye view, such as the drawing board affords, of how the whole thing is organised, though, in craft evolution, if not in software, the results have the appearance of natural organisms or of exceptionally well integrated designs. But there is an important difference: software is increasingly made by modifying the actual material of previous pieces of software, as a building may be altered for new use, whereas a waggon-maker, for instance, modifies the form, but does not re-use the material, in making each small step in the gradual evolution of his product.[25]

He clarifies his terms, noting, "I say 'making', not designing, because a programmer, unlike a designer in other fields, is himself both designer-and-maker; the medium of design is not a symbolic model of the product, it is the product itself."[26]

The implications of this transition in the nature of technology for design are profound. Psychologist David Canter notes:

Designing . . . helpful . . . software requires skills way beyond the three-dimensional design skills currently considered essential for an industrial designer. It especially needs a way of thinking about the product which is not limited to its physical, objective structure, nor even to the internal elegance of its software. It requires a creative grasp, an associated understanding of the whole set of interactions which are taking place between and within people and computers. As communication between computers and between people via computers increases, so this context will take on an increasingly social dimension — and so designers will need to shape social systems and provide means of social control to keep those people-computer interactions operating effectively. . . .

The new generation of computers is already demanding a new generation of skills. Development teams in industry are no longer staffed by people who have only engineering backgrounds. Psychologists, linguists, sociologists and such exotic breeds as ethnomusicologists and cultural anthropologists can be found amongst the systems analysts and software engineers.[27]

No firm criteria for judging the success of design in this new conception have yet been established, but some ideas are emerging. Jones, for example, writes, "I believe that one mark of good design in software, or anything else, is that of 'zero learning': the machine assumes one's best qualities, brings them out and enhances them. Then one can use it immediately, without special training, and reach 'beyond oneself'. Why Not?"[28] Elsewhere he amplifies this position:

Instead of instructing the machines to perform as if we are all fools we could begin to do the reverse. We could design the programs and the machines themselves so that they would not operate unless the users act as intelligently as they can. Instead of trying to make things work independently of people we could oblige them to depend on people to use all the discretion they have. Then, instead of fixing goals in advance, we could leave them to be worked out in the doing.[29]

When I asked Jones to further explain why he felt this to be necessary, he said:

It's mainly that we've accepted the idea that in order to live in the machine life we're going to be fools in a way, foolproof. "The people are hopeless," you know, and the machines are there to correct the defects of the people it seems. It's worse than that, you know, I think in any technological development I've been concerned with, I seem to detect this, that our self image is not good enough therefore the machine reflects our own poor view of ourselves.[30]

In reflecting on his many years of work on this topic, Jones, in his essay "The Future of Breathing," concludes:

THE SYSTEMS COULD BE "PEOPLE-DEPENDENT" . . . if the machine parts, and particularly software, are designed on this principle, and if computing power is completely decentralized, the thing would work BECAUSE of people, not IN SPITE of. No longer would designers try to make things "fool-proof". They'd have to find how to do the opposite.[31]

Here Jones addresses the essence of intangible design — a technology that exists, that is activated, *because* of peoples' needs and wishes, not in spite of them. The challenge is to find, as some are beginning to do, ways of bringing this about.

7. Depending on Everyone

I began this book by remarking on my surprise, and disappointment, at the lack of attention to user needs and wishes that I had found while a student of architecture. It is now becoming clear, in view of the large number of award-winning designs that have failed the test of use, that the design community's criteria for successful design differs radically from that of design users. Designers judge their work according to static, geometrical criteria born of their medium, two-dimensional scale drawings, while design users are concerned with the dynamic, experiential process of using things. The design approach that arose in response to industrialization — modernism — and the more recent reactions to it — postmodernism, late modernism, and deconstruction — have all proven insufficiently responsive to user wishes.

In the 1960s a range of design-research approaches developed outside the design professions in response to the perceived failure of mainstream design adequately to address the issues raised by industrialization. Design research, however, has had little impact and these approaches collectively have failed to improve designing. If anything, where techniques such as design methods were adopted they served to make design even more rigid, even less responsive to user wishes, than before.

Within the original design methods movement, however, were the seeds of a new, user-sensitive design. The two founders of the movement, John Chris Jones and Christopher Alexander, have each gone on to develop very advanced views of user-responsive design. Alexander developed a "pattern language" that enables users to shape their own environments. Jones, meanwhile, developed a view that design should be a response to the whole of life and need not always be directly linked with objects at all.

The work of Jones and Alexander suggests that design itself needs to be redefined in terms of peoples' experience, instead of in terms of objects. This static geometrical criteria of the design of the industrial era must be abandoned in favor of a focus on the dynamic, multisensory experiences of design users. Design must shift from a focus on products to a concern with processes. This transition in the conception of design is particularly important in application to newly emerging design tasks, such as the making of computer software, to which traditional techniques, such as design-by-drawing, are completely inapplicable.

As demonstrated, a number of design approaches have recently been developed in which user experience is, in one way or another, the focus. With collaborative design, for example, the designer's role in the design process changes and, as a consequence, the aims of designing itself change; a greater emphasis is placed on the "software" aspects of design — use, experience, and perception, than on the "hardware" aspect — physical form. Similarly, in contextual design the focus is on the creation of contexts for heightened perceptual experience, rather than on the formal properties of objects per se. The purpose of intangible design is to address the dynamic processes of experience and use at the systems level; for example, through the creation of technologies that work, as Jones suggests they should, *because* of people, not in spite of them.

I have been saying throughout this book that design is changing. This is perhaps inaccurate because, as seen from the many developments in design that have just been reviewed, it would be fairer to say design *has* changed. In a sense, then, this book is not so much a polemic as a history of the recent, if underrecognized, international trends toward more user-sensitive design. A philosophy through which a more user responsive design might develop in the future is set out in a manifesto by John Chris Jones.

> to begin with what can be imagined
> to use both intuition and reason
> to work it out in context
> to model the contextual effects of what is imagined
> to change the process to suit what is happening
> to refuse what diminishes
> to seek inspiration in what is
> to choose what depends upon everyone[1]

Depending on everyone necessitates designing at the scale of life itself — a collaboration on the broadest basis in which both contextual effects and intangible processes of use are of central, not secondary, importance in design.

NOTES

INTRODUCTION

1. See Charles Jencks, *The Language of Post-Modern Architecture,* 6th ed. (London: Academy Editions; New York: Rizzoli, 1991), 23.

2. See Paul Gapp, "An Analytical Return Visit to the Flawed But Spectacular State of Illinois Center," *Chicago Tribune,* 23 June 1985, sec. 13, p. 2, col. 2.

3. Paul Gapp, "Jahn's State of Illinois Center Revisited: Strong Enough to Survive the Storm," *Chicago Tribune,* 10 August 1986, sec. 13, p. 2, col. 2.

4. Ada Louise Huxtable, "A Landmark Before Its Doors Open," *New York Times,* 8 May 1977, sec. 2, p. 25, col. 1.

5. Stanley Abercrombie, "Bronx Developmental Center: A Much Honored Design Finally Begins the Test of Use," *Interiors* 138 (December 1978): 94.

6. Suzanne Stephens, "Role Models, the Individual: Richard Meier," *Progressive Architecture* 58 (May 1977): 61.

7. "Bronx Developmental Centre," *Architectural Review* 163 (February 1978): 96.

8. Paul Goldberger, "Masterwork or Nightmare?" *New York Times,* 3 May 1977, p. 43, col. 3.

9. Quoted in Suzanne Stephens, "Architecture Cross-Examined," *Progressive Architecture* 58 (July 1977): 53.

10. Richard Meier, *Richard Meier Architect* (New York: Rizzoli, 1984): 131.

11. "Bronx Developmental Center, New York City," *AIA Journal* 66 (May 1977): 36.

12. Quoted in Glenn Fowler, "Safety Risk Cited at Bronx Center for Retarded," *New York Times,* 2 December 1980, sec. 2, p. 1, col. 3.

13. Huxtable, "A Landmark Before Its Doors Open," p. 25, col. 1.

14. Stephens, "Architecture Cross-Examined," 52–53.

15. Ibid., 43–44.

16. Goldberger, "Masterwork or Nightmare?" p. 43, col. 3.

17. Abercrombie, "Bronx Developmental Center," 97.

18. Huxtable, "A Landmark Before Its Doors Open," sec. 2, p. 25, col. 1.

19. "New Center for Disabled is Focus of Philosophical Controversy," *Industrial Design* 24 (July 1977): 14.

20. Goldberger, "Masterwork or Nightmare?" p. 43, col. 3.

21. Abercrombie, "Bronx Developmental Center," 92.

22. Ibid., 93–97.

23. Quoted in Suzanne Stephens, "Architecture Cross-Examined," 54.

24. Fowler, "Safety Risk Cited," sec. 1, p. 1, col. 3.

25. Ibid.

26. "Bronx Developmental Center, New York City," 36.

27. Fowler, "Safety Risk Cited," sec. 2, p. 1, col. 3.

28. "The Bronx Developmental Center," *AIA Journal* 67 (mid-May 1978): 146.

29. Stephens, "Architecture Cross-Examined," 51.

30. Meier, *Richard Meier Architect*, 143.

31. Stephens, "Architecture Cross-Examined," 51.

32. Ibid., 54.

33. Tom Wolfe, *From Bauhaus to Our House* (New York: Farrar, Straus and Giroux, 1981).

34. See H.R.H. The Prince of Wales, *A Vision of Britain: A Personal View of Architecture* (London: Doubleday, 1989).

PART 1: DESIGN IN TRANSITION

1. Andrea Branzi, *The Hot House: Italian New Wave Design* (Milan: Idea Books; London: Thames and Hudson, 1984), 142.

2. Ibid., 87.

3. Andrea Branzi, *Learning from Milan: Design and the Second Modernity* (Milan: Idea Books, 1988; Cambridge, Mass.: The MIT Press, 1988), 18.

4. John Thackara, "Beyond the Object in Design," in *Design After Modernism: Beyond the Object*, ed. John Thackara (London: Thames and Hudson, 1988), 11–34.

5. Charles L. Owen, "Design Education in the Information Age," *Design Processes Newsletter* 3, no. 3 (1989).

6. Bill Evans, "The Japanese Corporate Approach," in *Design Management: A Handbook of Issues and Methods*, ed. Mark Oakley (Oxford, England, and Cambridge, Mass.: Blackwell Research, 1990), 306.

7. William Morris, "How We Live and How We Might Live," in *News from Nowhere and Selected Writings and Designs*, ed. Asa Briggs (Harmondsworth, England: Penguin, 1984), 177.

8. Charles Jencks, *The Language of Post-Modern Architecture*, 5th ed. (London: Academy Editions; New York: Rizzoli, 1987), 5.

1. DESIGN PHILOSOPHIES SINCE INDUSTRIALIZATION

1. William Morris, "Innate Socialism," in *News from Nowhere and Selected Writings and Designs,* ed. Asa Briggs (Harmondsworth, England: Penguin, 1984), 104.

2. Walter Gropius, *New Architecture and the Bauhaus* (Cambridge, Mass.: MIT Press, 1965), 34–37.

3. Ibid., 38, 90–91.

4. Ibid., 19–20.

5. Le Corbusier, *Towards a New Architecture*, trans. Frederick Etchells (London: Architectural Press, 1927; New York: Praeger, 1960), 12–13.

6. Ibid., 7.

7. David Byrne, *True Stories* (London: Faber and Faber; New York: Viking Penguin, 1986), 30.

8. Quoted in Kenneth Frampton, *Modern Architecture: A Critical History* (London: Thames and Hudson, 1985), 116–117.

9. Nikolaus Pevsner, *Pioneers of Modern Design: From William Morris to Walter Gropius* (Harmondsworth, England: Penguin, 1975), 214–215.

10. Andrea Branzi, *The Hot House: Italian New Wave Design* (Milan: Idea Books; London: Thames and Hudson, 1984), 33.

11. Le Corbusier, *Towards a New Architecture*, 14.

12. Robert Hughes, *The Shock of the New* (New York: Alfred A. Knopf, 1987), 165.

13. Ibid., 167–68.

14. Ibid., 165.

15. Quoted in Ibid., 165.

16. Tom Wolfe, *From Bauhaus to Our House* (New York: Farrar, Straus and Giroux, 1981), 32.

17. Quoted in Diane Raines Ward, "Happy 100th Corbu," *Connoisseur* 217 (February 1987): 28.

18. Quoted in Philip C. Johnson, ed., *Mies van der Rohe* (New York: Museum of Modern Art, 1947), 186–187.

19. See Frank Lloyd Wright, *Genius and the Mobocracy* (New York: Horizon Press, 1949).

20. John Thackara "Beyond the Object in Design," in *Design After Modernism: Beyond the Object*, ed. John Thackara (London: Thames and Hudson, 1988), 11.

21. Ada Louise Huxtable, "The Troubled State of Modern Architecture," *Architectural Design* 51, nos. 1–2 (1981): 9.

22. Ibid.

23. Ibid., 10.

24. Charles Jencks, *The Language of Post-Modern Architecture*, 5th ed. (London: Academy Editions; New York: Rizzoli, 1987), 6.

25. Robert Venturi, *Complexity and Contradiction in Architecture* (New York: Museum of Modern Art, 1966), 22, 23.

26. Ibid., 48-49, 102.

27. Robert Venturi, Denise Scott Brown, and Steven Izenour, *Learning from Las Vegas* (Cambridge, Mass.: MIT Press, 1972), 87.

28. Ibid., 106.

29. John Chris Jones, *Design Methods*, 2nd ed. (New York: Van Nostrand Reinhold, 1992), xxx.

30. Robert Venturi, Denise Scott Brown, and Steve Izenour. *Learning from Las Vegas* (Cambridge, Mass.: MIT Press, 1972), 108.

31. Wolfe, *From Bauhaus to Our House*, 98, 100.

32. Venturi, *Complexity and Contradiction*, 116.

33. Jencks, *Post-Modern Architecture*, 88.

34. Venturi, *Complexity and Contradiction*, 14.

35. Peter Eisenman, *House X* (New York: Rizzoli, 1982), 34.

36. Charles Jencks, *Late Modern Architecture* (New York: Rizzoli, 1980), 8.

37. Suzanne Stephens, "Role Models, The Individual: Richard Meier," *Progressive Architecture* 58 (May 1977): 61.

38. Quoted in Charles Jencks, "Perennial Architectural Debate," *Architectural Design* 53, no. 7–8 (1983): 5.

39. Peter Eisenman, "The End of the Classical," *Perspecta* 21 (1984).

40. Quoted in Roger Kimball, "The Death and Resurrection of Postmodern Architecture," *New Criterion* 6 (June 1988): 25.

41. Roger Kimball, *Tenured Radicals* (New York: Harper and Row, 1990), 124–125.

42. Kimball, *Tenured Radicals*, 130.

43. David Clarke, *Frank Lloyd Wright and the Laffer Curve* (Wolfeboro, N.H., and London: Longwood Academic Press). Forthcoming in 1992.

44. "Peter Eisenman: An Architectural Design Interview by Charles Jencks," *Architectural Design* 59, nos. 3–4 (1989): 50.

45. Ibid., 56.

46. Ibid., 52.

47. Kimball, *Tenured Radicals*, 119.

48. Charles Jencks, "Deconstruction: The Pleasures of Absence," *Architectural Design*, vol. 58, nos. 3–4 (1988): 17, 22.

49. "Architect as Non-Hero," *Architects' Journal*, no. 171 (3 May 1980): 471.

50. Venturi, Scott Brown, and Izenour, *Learning from Las Vegas*, x–xi.

51. Andrea Branzi, *Learning from Milan: Design and the Second Modernity* (Milan: Idea Books; Cambridge, Mass.: MIT Press, 1988), 25.

52. Ibid., 69.

53. Ibid., 29.

54. Clarke, *Frank Lloyd Wright*, Forthcoming in 1992.

55. Christopher Alexander, "Letter to the Editor," *Progressive Architecture* 71 (April 1990): 11.

56. "Contrasting Concepts of Harmony in Architecture: Debate Between Christopher Alexander and Peter Eisenman," *Lotus International* 40 (1983): 61.

57. Venturi, Scott Brown, and Izenour, *Learning from Las Vegas* , 106.

58. Venturi, *Complexity and Contradiction*, 52.

59. Clarke, *Frank Lloyd Wright*, Forthcoming in 1992.

60. Andrea Branzi, *The Hot House: Italian New Wave Design*. (Milan: Idea Books; London: Thames and Hudson, 1984), 147.

2. DESIGN RESEARCH

1. Henry Sanoff and Sidney Cohn, Preface to *ERDA 1: Proceedings of the 1st Annual Environmental Design Research Association Conference*, ed. Henry Sanoff and Sidney Cohn (Stroudsburg, Penn.: Dowden, Hutchinson, and Ross, 1970), vi.

2. Robert Sommer "Research on Utilization: Did Anyone Use It? Where Did We Lose It?" in *Coming of Age: EDRA 21/1990*, Robert I. Selby et al, eds. (Oklahoma City, Okla.: EDRA, 1990), 4.

3. Christopher Alexander, *Notes on the Synthesis of Form* (Cambridge, Mass.: Harvard University Press, 1964), 1, 3–5.

4. Ibid., 5.

5. Ibid., 16.

6. John Chris Jones, *Design Methods*, 2nd ed. (New York: Van Nostrand Reinhold, 1992), 30–31.

7. J. Christopher Jones, "Trying to Design the Future," *Design*, no. 223 (September 1967): 35–36.

8. Jones, *Design Methods*, 20.

9. J. Christopher Jones, "Design Methods Reviewed," in *The Design Method*, ed. S. A. Gregory (New York: Plenum Press, 1966), 298.

10. John Chris Jones and C. Thomas Mitchell, "Conversation Transcripts," 1989.

11. John Chris Jones, "Activities, Artifacts and Concepts: Some Thoughts on the Singularities of Modern Life," 1957

12. Ibid.

13. Ibid.

14. Jones, *Design Methods*, 20.

15. Ibid.

16. John Chris Jones, *Designing Designing* (London: Architecture, Design and Technology Press, 1991), 133.

17. Jones and Mitchell, "Conversation Transcripts."

18. See Constantinos A. Doxiadis, *Architecture in Transition* (New York: Oxford University Press, 1963), 77.

19. Alexander, *Notes on the Synthesis of Form*, 10–11.

20. Alexander, *Notes on the Synthesis of Form*, 68–70.

21. Ibid., 75, 77.

22. Ibid., 21, 77.

23. Ibid., 70.

24. Jones, *Designing Designing*, 78–79.

25. Jones, *Design Methods*, 9.

26. Jones and Mitchell, "Conversation Transcripts."

27. Jones, *Design Methods*, 236, 244, 224.

28. Ibid., 45.

29. J. Christopher Jones, "Design Methods Compared 2: Tactics," *Design*, no. 213 (September 1966): 45.

30. Christopher L. Crickmay in collaboration with J. Christopher Jones, *Design I: Imagination and Method: Designing as a Response to Life as a Whole* (Bletchley, Buckinghamshire, England: Open University Press, 1972), 10.

31. Jones and Mitchell, "Conversation Transcripts."

32. Crickmay and Jones, *Design I*, 9.

33. Ibid.

34. J. Christopher Jones. "An Experiment in Education for Planning and Design." in *Emerging Methods in Environmental Design and Planning*, ed. Gary T. Moore (Cambridge, Mass.: MIT Press, 1970), 353–54.

35. Jones, *Design Methods*, 61-62.

36. Jones, *Designing Designing*, 39.

37. Alexander, *Notes on the Synthesis of Form*, 84.

38. Jones. "An Experiment in Education," 353–354.

39. Jones, *Design Methods*, xxiii.

40. Ibid., 323–24.

41. Ibid., 339.

42. Jones, "Design Methods Reviewed," 308.

43. J. Christopher Jones, "A Method of Systematic Design," in *Conference on Design Methods*, ed. J. C. Jones and D. G. Thornley (Oxford, England: Pergamon Press, 1963), 64.

44. Jones, *Designing Designing*, 158–59, 163.

45. Ibid., 174, 182.

46. Ibid., 159.

47. Christopher Alexander, "The State of the Art in Design Methodology (replies to questions by M. Jacobson)," *DMG Newsletter*, March 1971, 3–7.

48. "Contrasting Concepts of Harmony in Architecture: Debate between Christopher Alexander and Peter Eisenman," *Lotus International* 40 (1983): 61–63.

49. Christopher Alexander et al, *A Pattern Language* (New York: Oxford University Press, 1977).

50. Christopher Alexander, *The Timeless Way of Building* (New York: Oxford University Press, 1979), x.

51. Ibid., 62, 65, 70, 72.

52. Ibid., 74.

53. Ibid., 167, 225, 246.

54. Ibid., 231–232, 235–36.

55. Ibid., 239.

56. Ibid., 479–480, 485.

57. Ibid., 525–526.

58. Ibid., 531, 544–45.

59. Jones, *Designing Designing*, 31, 32–33.

60. Jones, *Design Methods*, xxvii.

61. Jones, *Designing Designing*, 149, 152, 180, 181.

62. Jones and Mitchell, "Conversation Transcripts"

63. Ibid.

64. See Jones, *Designing Designing*, ix.

65. Ibid., ix, xxi.

66. Jones, *Design Methods*, xxii.

67. Jones, *Designing Designing*, 26–27.

68. Ibid., 115–16.

69. Ibid., 107.

70. Ibid., 120–21.

71. Jones, *Design Methods*, xxv.

3. FROM PRODUCT TO PROCESS DESIGN

1. John Chris Jones, *Designing Designing* (London: Architecture, Design and Technology Press, 1991), 206.

2. Ibid., 79.

3. John Chris Jones, *Design Methods*, 2nd ed. (New York: Van Nostrand Reinhold, 1992), 4.

4. Ibid., 6.

5. Christopher Alexander, *Notes on the Synthesis of Form* (Cambridge, Mass.: Harvard University Press, 1964), 15.

6. Jones, *Design Methods*, xxviii–xxix.

7. Christopher L. Crickmay in collaboration with J. Christopher Jones, *Design I: Imagination and Method: Designing as a Response to Life as a Whole* (Bletchley, Buckinghamshire, England: The Open University Press, 1972), 7.

8. Quoted in Suzanne Stephens, "Architecture Cross-Examined," *Progressive Architecture* 58 (July 1977): 54.

9. Jones, *Designing Designing*, ix–x.

10. Ibid., ix.

11. Jones, *Design Methods*, xxv–xxvi.

12. Ibid., xxviii.

13. Ibid., xxvi.

14. Ralph Caplan in *Connections: The Work of Charles and Ray Eames* (Los Angeles: UCLA Arts Council, 1976), 32–33.

15. Andrea Branzi, *The Hot House: Italian New Wave Design* (Milan: Idea Books; London: Thames and Hudson, 1984), 58-60.

16. Christopher Alexander, *The Timeless Way of Building* (New York: Oxford University Press, 1979), 91.

17. Ibid., 159.

18. Ibid., 364.

19. Jones, *Designing Designing*, 162.

20. Alan W. Watts, *The Way of Zen* (New York: Pantheon, 1957), 5.

21. Jones, *Designing Designing*, 212.

22. Jones, *Design Methods*, xxvii.

23. Ibid., xxx.

24. Jones, *Designing Designing*, 65.

PART 2: DESIGN TURNED INSIDE OUT

1. John Chris Jones, *Designing Designing* (London: Architecture, Design and Technology Press, 1991), 80.

4. COLLABORATIVE ENVIRONMENTAL DESIGN

1. John Chris Jones, *Design Methods,* 2nd ed. (New York: Van Nostrand Reinhold, 1992), xxvii.

2. Henry David Thoreau, *The Illustrated Walden* (Princeton, N.J.: Princeton University Press, 1973), 47.

3. Quoted in Tom Mitchell, "New Housing Design Tried in East Wahdat," *Jordan Times,* 21 September 1983: 5.

4. Quoted in C. Thomas Mitchell, "An Analysis of the Conference Headquarters Office," unpublished report of the Center for Design Process, 1990.

5. See "Ralph Erskine: The Humane Architect," in *AD Profiles 9,* ed. Mats Egelius, 1977, 11-12.

6. Colin Amery, "Byker by Erskine," *Architectural Review,* 156 (December 1974): 360.

7. Ibid., 361.

8. Peter Malpass, "A Reappraisal of Byker, Part 1: Magic, Myth and the Architect—The Other Side of the Wall," *Architects' Journal,* 9 May 1979, 968.

9. Amery, "Byker by Erskine," 362.

10. Charles Jencks, *The Language of Post-Modern Architecture,* 6th ed. (London: Academy Editions; New York: Rizzoli, 1991), 86.

11. Lucien Kroll, "Soft Zone," *Architectural Association Quarterly 7,* no. 4 (1975): 52.

12. Geoffrey Broadbent, "Educating Designers," in *Changing Design,* Barrie Evans et al., eds. (London: David Fulton Publishers, 1982), 182.

13. Ibid., 186.

14. Christopher Alexander, *The Timeless Way of Building* (New York: Oxford University Press, 1979), 354.

15. Jencks, *Post-Modern Architecture,* 86.

16. Alexander, *The Timeless Way of Building,* 164.

17. John Chris Jones, *Designing Designing* (London: Architecture, Design and Technology Press, 1991), 205.

18. John Chris Jones, "Softecnica," in *Design After Modernism: Beyond the Object,* ed. John Thackara (London: Thames and Hudson, 1988), 225.

5. CONTEXTUAL DESIGN

1. John Chris Jones, *Design Methods,* 2nd ed. (New York: Van Nostrand Reinhold, 1992), xxx.

2. Robert Venturi, Denise Scott Brown, and Steven Izenour, *Learning from Las Vegas* (Cambridge, Mass.: MIT Press, 1972), 87.

3. J. Christopher Jones, "Automation and Design 5," *Design*, no. 110 (February 1958): 44.

4. John Thackara, "Designing without Form," *Design*, no. 440 (August 1985): 39.

5. Julian Gibb, "Soft: An Appeal to Common Senses," *Design*, no. 433 (January 1985): 28.

6. Andrea Branzi, *The Hot House: Italian New Wave Design* (Milan: Idea Books; London: Thames and Hudson, 1984), 97–100.

7. Ibid., 100.

8. John Howell, "Reviews: Robert Wilson and David Byrne: the Knee Plays," *Artforum* 25 (March 1987): 131.

9. Ibid.

10. Janny Donker, *The President of Paradise: A Traveller's Account of Robert Wilson's CIVIL warS* (Amsterdam: International Theatre Bookshop, 1985), 23–24.

11. Ibid., 32.

12. Dale Harris, "Robert Wilson's Epic Vision," *Connoisseur* 214 (April 1984): 103.

13. Franco Quadri, "Robert Wilson: It's About Time," *Artforum* 22 (October 1984): 79, 82.

14. John Howell, "Forum: What Becomes a Legend Most," *Artforum* 23 (March 1985): 90.

15. Melissa Harris, "Reviews: Robert Wilson: Brooklyn Academy of Music," *Flash Art*, March 1985, 44.

16. Dale Harris, "Robert Wilson's Epic Vision," *Connoisseur* 214 (April 1984): 105.

17. David Byrne, *True Stories* (London: Faber and Faber; New York: Viking Penguin, 1986), 9.

18. Jill Johnston, "Family Spectacles," *Art in America* 74 (December 1986): 95.

19. Robert Wilson, "Robert Wilson," *International Design*, September–October 1984, 41.

20. Ibid.

21. Ibid.

22. "Christo: The Pont-Neuf Wrapped, Paris, 1975–1985," press release.

23. Charlotte Ellis, "Pont Neuf Under Wraps," *RIBA Journal* 92 (November 1985): 11.

24. Michael Spens, "Comment: Christo's Wrappings," *Studio International* 198 (December 1985): 2.

25. Jonathan Kuhn, "The Picasso Museum, Christo's Pont Neuf Project, and Pei's Pyramid: Reflections on Artistic Ego and the Artistic Life of Paris," *Arts Magazine* 61 (December 1986): 92.

26. Ibid.

27. Werner Spies, Introduction to *Christo Prints and Objects, 1963–1987*, ed. Jörg Schellmann and Joséphine Benecke (Munich: Edition Schellmann; New York: Abbeville Press, 1988), 14.

28. "Christo: Running Fence, Sonoma and Marin Counties, 1972–76," press release.

29. "Christo: Surrounded Islands, Biscayne Bay, Greater Miami, Florida, 1980–83," press release.

30. "Christo: Surrounded Islands, Biscayne Bay, Greater Miami, Florida, 1980–83," press release.

31. "The Umbrellas, Joint Project for Japan and U.S.A.," press release.

32. Quoted in Vicki Linder, "Sculpture: The Arts," *Omni* 4 (July 1982): 112.

33. Spies in *Christo Prints and Objects*, 12.

34. David Bourdon, "Artist's Dialogue: A Conversation with Christo," *Architectural Digest* 38 (November 1981): 194.

35. David Bourdon, *Christo* (New York: Harry N. Abrams, n.d.), 36.

36. Spies in *Christo Prints and Objects*, 10.

37. Quoted in Linder, "Sculpture," 112.

38. Lisa Licitra Ponti, "Conversazione con Christo: On Running Fence Project," *Domus*, no. 549 (August 1975): 54.

39. Maudette Ball, "Documenting Evanescent Projects," *Artweek*, 19 December 1981, 3.

40. Jonathan Fineberg, "Theater of the Real: Thoughts on Christo," *Art in America* 67 (December 1979): 99.

41. Lawrence Alloway, *Christo* (New York: Harry N. Abrams, 1969), vi.

42. Ibid., viii.

43. Ibid., vii.

44. Brian Eno, interview with author, 25 July 1991.

45. Jacki Apple, "Spotlight Review," *High Performance*, Spring 1989, 52.

46. Quoted in Brian Eno and Russell Mills, *More Dark Than Shark* (London: Faber and Faber, 1986), 41.

47. Ibid., 73.

48. Brian Eno, *Discreet Music* (Editions E. G., 1975).

49. Brian Eno, *Ambient 1: Music for Airports* (E. G. Records, 1978).

50. Brian Eno, interview with author, 25 July 1991.

51. Ibid.

52. Ibid.

53. Ibid.

54. Quoted in Rick Poynor, "Landscape Dreamer," *Designers' Journal*, October 1987, 56.

55. Brian Eno, interview with author, 25 July 1991.

56. Ibid.

57. Ibid.

58. Ibid.

59. Ibid.

60. Ibid.

61. Ibid.

62. J. Christopher Jones, *Writings Remembered* (Self-published, 1976).

63. John Chris Jones and C. Thomas Mitchell, "Conversation Transcripts," 1989.

6. INTANGIBLE DESIGN

1. John Chris Jones, *Design Methods*, 2nd ed. (New York: Van Nostrand Reinhold, 1992), xxvi.

2. John Chris Jones, *Designing Designing* (London: Architecture, Design and Technology Press, 1991), 134.

3. Lao Tzu, *Tao Teh Ching*, trans. John C. H. Wu (Boston: Shambhala, 1989), 23.

4. Stephen W. Draper and Donald A. Norman, Introduction to *User Centered System Design: New Perspectives on Human-Computer Interaction*, ed. Donald A. Norman and Stephen W. Draper (Hillsdale, N.J.: Lawrence Erlbaum Associates, 1986), 2.

5. Ibid.

6. Quoted in Dick Powell, "The Human Road Ahead," *Design* 407 (November 1982): 38.

7. "Digitised Sighs," *The Economist*, 4 August 1990, 68.

8. Sheridan M. Tatsuno, *Created in Japan: From Imitators to World-Class Innovators* (New York: Harper and Row, 1990), 263.

9. Ibid., 270.

10. John Rheinfrank, interview with author, 20 March 1991.

11. Ibid.

12. Ibid.

13. Ibid.

14. John Rheinfrank, Katherine A. Welker, and Stuart K. Card, "Situated Languages for the Design of Computer-Human Interfaces," n.d.

15. Ibid.

16. John Rheinfrank, interview with author, 20 March 1991.

17. Ibid.

18. Ibid.

19. Rheinfrank, Welker, and Card, "Situated Languages."

20. John Chris Jones, "Softecnica," in *Design After Modernism: Beyond the Object*, ed. John Thackara (London: Thames and Hudson, 1988), 216.

21. J. David Bolter, *Turing's Man: Western Culture in the Computer Age* (Chapel Hill: University of North Carolina Press, 1984), 39–40.

22. Jones, "Softecnica," 216–217.

23. Bolter, *Turing's Man*, 17.

24. Ibid., 166.

25. Jones, *Designing Designing*, 197.

26. Ibid., 193.

27. David Canter, "From Knobs and Dials to Knowledge," *Design*, no. 428 (August 1984): 31–33.

28. Jones, "Softecnica," 219.

29. John Chris Jones, "Depending on Everyone: Some Thoughts on Contextual Design," *Design Studies* 11, no. 4 (October 1990): 193.

30. John Chris Jones and C. Thomas Mitchell, "Conversation Transcripts," 1989.

31. Jones, *Designing Designing*, xxxviii.

7. DEPENDING ON EVERYONE

1. John Chris Jones, "Depending on Everyone: Some Thoughts on Contextual Design," *Design Studies* 11, no. 4 (October 1990): 187.

LIST OF ILLUSTRATIONS

PAGE 17. Philip Johnson. Glass House, New Canaan, Connecticut, 1949. (Photo: Ezra Stoller. Courtesy of Philip Johnson.)

PAGE 18. Philip Johnson and John Burgee. AT&T Corporate Headquarters, New York, 1983. (Photo: Timothy Hursley. Courtesy of Philip Johnson.)

PAGE 19, top. Venturi and Rauch. Tucker House, Katonah, New York, 1975. Exterior View. (Photo: Tom Crane. Courtesy of Venturi, Scott Brown and Associates.)

PAGE 19, bottom. Venturi and Rauch. Tucker House, Katonah, New York, 1975. Interior View. (Photo: Tom Crane. Courtesy of Venturi, Scott Brown and Associates.)

PAGE 20. Venturi and Rauch in collaboration with Cope and Lippencott. Guild House, Philadelphia, 1963. (Photo: William Watkins. Courtesy of Venturi, Scott Brown and Associates.)

PAGE 22. Peter Eisenman. House IV, 1971. Transformational Diagrams. (From Peter Eisenman. *House X*. New York: Rizzoli, 1982. Reprinted courtesy of Eisenman Architects.)

PAGE 23, top. Peter Eisenman. House III, 1970. Axonometric View. (From Peter Eisenman. *House X*. New York: Rizzoli, 1982. Reprinted courtesy of Eisenman Architects.)

PAGE 23, bottom. Peter Eisenman. House III for Robert Miller. Lakeville, Connecticut, 1971. Exterior View. (Photo: Dick Frank. Courtesy of Eisenman Architects.)

PAGE 24. Peter Eisenman. House VI for the Franks. Cornwall, Connecticut, 1975. Interior View. (Photo: Dick Frank. Courtesy of Eisenman Architects.)

PAGE 25. Peter Eisenman. House VI for the Franks. Cornwall, Connecticut, 1975. Interior View. (Photo: Dick Frank. Courtesy of Eisenman Architects.)

PAGE 27. Peter Eisenman. Project for Cannaregio Town Square. Venice, Italy, 1980. (Photo: Dick Frank. Courtesy of Eisenman Architects.)

2. DESIGN RESEARCH

PAGE 48. Christopher Alexander. Tree Diagram. (Reprinted by permission of the publishers from *Notes on the Synthesis of Form,* by Christopher Alexander, Cambridge, Mass.: Harvard University Press, Copyright © 1964 by the President and Fellows of Harvard College.)

PAGE 94. Robert Wilson. Drawing, Sketch, and Performance View for Knee Play 6. From the *Knee Plays* by Robert Wilson and David Byrne from *the CIVIL warS: a tree is best measured when it is down* by Robert Wilson. (Drawing is in the BankAmerica Collection, San Francisco (#85174.) Photograph courtesy of Paula Cooper Gallery, New York. Sketch by Robert Wilson, courtesy Byrd Hoffman Foundation, Inc. Performance: Produced by Walker Art Center. Photo courtesy Walker Art Center.)

PAGE 97. Christo. The Pont-Neuf Wrapped, Project for Paris. Collage in 2 Parts, 1983. (Photo: Wolfgang Volz. Copyright: Christo, 1983.)

PAGE 98. Christo. The Pont-Neuf Wrapped, Project for Paris, 1975–85. (Photo: Wolfgang Volz. Copyright: Christo, 1985.)

PAGE 99, top. Christo. The Pont-Neuf Wrapped, Project for Paris, 1975–85. Painted Photograph, 1984. (Photo: Wolfgang Volz. Copyright: Christo, 1984.)

PAGE 99, bottom. Christo. The Pont-Neuf Wrapped, Project for Paris, 1975–85. (Photo: Wolfgang Volz. Copyright: Christo, 1985.)

PAGE 100. Christo. The Pont-Neuf Wrapped, Project for Paris, 1975–85. (Photo: Eeva Inkeri. Copyright: Christo, 1985.)

PAGE 101. Christo. Running Fence, Sonoma and Marin Counties, California, 1972–76. (Photo copyright: Wolfgang Volz. Copyright: Christo, 1976.)

PAGE 102, top. Christo. Running Fence, Sonoma and Marin Counties, California. Collage, 1975. (Photo: Eeva-Inkeri. Copyright: Christo, 1975.)

PAGE 102, bottom. Christo. Running Fence, Sonoma and Marin Counties, California, 1972–76. (Photo: Wolfgang Volz. Copyright: Christo, 1976.)

PAGE 103. Christo. Surrounded Islands, Project for Biscayne Bay, Greater Miami, Florida. 1980-83. (Photo: Copyright: Wolfgang Volz. Copyright: Christo, 1983.)

PAGE 104. Christo and Jeanne-Claude Christo during the staking for "The Umbrellas, Joint Project for Japan and U.S.A." October 1988, Ibaraki, Japan. (Photo copyright: Wolfgang Volz, 1988.)

PAGE 105. Christo. The Umbrellas, Joint Project for Japan and U.S.A. Collage in 2 Parts, 1990. (Photo: Wolfgang Volz. Copyright: Christo, 1990.)

PAGE 106. Christo. The Umbrellas, Joint Project for Japan and U.S.A. Collage in 2 Parts, 1990. (Photo: Wolfgang Volz. Copyright: Christo, 1990.)

PAGE 109. Portrait of Brian Eno (London, 1987.) (Photo: Maria Vedder, insert from: "VENICE 5" Design: Kevin Cann, courtesy Atelier Markgraph GmbH, Frankfurt. © Opal Information.)

PAGE 110. Brian Eno. Operational Diagram for "Discreet Music." (Courtesy of Brian Eno.)

PAGE 111. Brian Eno. Scores for Ambient 1: Music for Airports. (Courtesy of Brian Eno.)

6. INTANGIBLE DESIGN

PAGE 123. Exploratory Design Lab. Presentation from "Learning and Technology: new perspectives" project for Apple Computer. (Courtesy of Fitch RichardsonSmith.)

PAGE 124. Exploratory Design Lab. Interactive windows on Xerox 5046 photocopier. (Photo: Kevin Hutchinson.)

PAGE 126. Exploratory Design Lab. "Animating Interfaces" project presentation. (Courtesy of Fitch RichardsonSmith.)

SOURCE ACKNOWLEDGMENTS

Excerpts from "Safety Risk Cited at Bronx Center for Retarded," by Glenn Fowler, Dec. 2, 1980; "A Landmark Before Its Doors Open," by Ada Louise Huxtable, May 8, 1977; and "Masterwork or Nightmare?" by Paul Goldberger, May 3, 1977, copyright © 1977/80 The New York Times Company; reprinted by permission.

Excerpts from *Progressive Architecture* reprinted courtesy of Penton Publishing.

Excerpts from *Architectural Review* and *The Architects' Journal* reprinted courtesy of the Architectural Press.

Excerpts from "Bronx Developmental Center, New York City," *AIA Journal*, vol. 66, May 1977 and "Bronx Developmental Center," *AIA Journal*, vol. 67, Mid-May 1978, copyright.© BPI Communications, Inc.

Excerpts from *The Language of Post-Modern Architecture* by Charles Jencks reprinted courtesy of Academy Editions, London.

Le Corbusier excerpts: Reprinted by permission of Greenwood Publishing Group, Inc., Westport, CT from *Towards a New Architecture* by Le Corbusier. Translated by Frederick Etchells. Also by permission of the Architectural Press.

Excerpts from *The Shock of the New* by Robert Hughes copyright © Robert Hughes, 1980; reprinted by permission of Alfred A. Knopf Publishers.

Excerpts from BAUHAUS TO OUR HOUSE by Tom Wolfe, copyright © 1981 by Tom Wolfe; reprinted by permission of Farrar, Straus and Giroux, Inc., and by permission of International Creative Management, Inc.

Material from *Architectural Design*: vol. 51, issue 1/2 (1981): 9–10; vol. 59, issue 3/4 (1989): 50, 52, and 56; and vol. 58, issue 3/4 (1988): 17 and 22, reproduced courtesy of *Architectural Design* Magazine, London.

INDEX

Note: page numbers in italics refer to illustrations

Printed in the United Kingdom
by Lightning Source UK Ltd.
100789UKS00001B/19-28